D0715647

The Longest Aisle

Our very own blushing bride, Claudia Sherman.

The Longest Aisle

An Offbeat Guide to Wedding Planning

Richard Mintzer

A CITADEL PRESS BOOK
Published by Carol Publishing Group

Copyright © 1994 by Richard Mintzer
Interior illustrations by Amy Cyphers

All rights reserved. No part of this book may be reproduced in any form, except by a newspaper or magazine reviewer who wishes to quote brief passages in connection with a review.

A Citadel Press Book
Published by Carol Publishing Group
Citadel Press is a registered trademark of Carol Communications, Inc.

Editorial Offices: 600 Madison Avenue, New York, N.Y. 10022
Sales and Distribution Offices: 120 Enterprise Avenue, Secaucus, N.J. 07094
In Canada: Canadian Manda Group, P.O. Box 920, Station U, Toronto, Ontario M8Z 5P9
Queries regarding rights and permissions should be addressed to
Carol Publishing Group, 600 Madison Avenue, New York, N.Y. 10022

Carol Publishing Group books are available at special discounts for bulk purchases, sales promotions, fundraising, or educational purposes.
Special editions can be created to specifications. For details contact: Special Sales Department, Carol Publishing Group, 120 Enterprise Avenue, Secaucus, N.J. 07094

Manufactured in the United States of America
10 9 8 7 6 5 4 3 2 1

Library of Congress Cataloging-in-Publication Data

Mintzer Richard.
   The longest aisle : an offbeat guide to wedding planning /
by Richard Mintzer.
       p.   cm.
   ISBN 0-8065-1575-9 (pbk.)
   1. Wedding etiquette.   2. Weddings—Planning.   I. Title.
BJ2051.M56   1994
395'.22'0207—dc20   94-20506
                                                      CIP

Photos by Phil Nee
Featuring comedienne Claudia Sherman as the bride

The Longest Aisle is lovingly dedicated to my wife, Carol, with whom I walked the aisle in 1988 and would gladly do it again today. Guests remember that on the return trip from the altar—the recessional—the keyboard player (at my request) played the theme from "The Odd Couple." Anything for a laugh.

Contents

Preface *xi*

1 Getting Married: What It's All About *1*
Love and Marriage
The Meaning of Commitment
The Changing Face of Weddings
Famous Marriages Made Just Short of Heaven
Wedding Quiz
Common Questions and Answers

2 The First Steps *15*
Proposals
Engagements: A Time to Prepare
Short Versus Long Engagements
Buying the Ring(s)
Engagement Parties
Scheduling the Big Event
The Wedding Calendar
The High Cost of Putting It All Together: Who Pays?
Money-Saving Tips
The Wedding Expert
Bridal Magazines
Eight Different Ways to Wed
Customs

3 The Big Steps *46*
Reception Sites
The Caterer
Whom You Should and Shouldn't Have in Your Bridal Party

A Bride's Guide to Wearing White
Buying the Ultimate Dress
A Few Words About Headpieces
A Very Few Words About Accessories
Ladies' Shopping Day
Tuxedo Rental Day
The Wedding Gift Registry: Making It Work for You
The Guest List
Invitations
The Seating Plan
Waiting for the Photos
The Photographer
Videotaping the Wedding: Finding the Right "Video Guy"
Finding the Wedding Band or DJ
The Flowers
The Cake
Limousines
Attendants' Gifts

4 The Final Steps   119
The Marriage License
Bridal Showers and Bachelorette Parties
The Bachelor Party
Prenuptials
Rehearsals
Cold Feet
Imperfect Weddings
Wedding Glitches

5 The Moment of Truth   139
The Vows
Exchanging Rings
A Plethora of Toasts
The Name Game
Getting Remarried

6 Over the Threshold   150
Honeymoons
Planning the Honeymoon
How to Know When the Honeymoon Is Definitely Over

7   **Settling Down**   *160*
    Thank-You Notes
    The Ten Most Important Newlywed Rules
    Furnishing The Newlyweds' Home
    Friends: Getting to Know Them
    The First Fight
    Money and the Newlyweds

8   **Addendum**   *172*
    Odds and Ends
    A Wedding Review: A Quiz
    Wedding Jokes

    Glossary: A Few Wedding Terms You Should Know   *177*

Preface

The Longest Aisle is designed to assist anyone along the way to the altar. No, it may not help you make all your impending and important plans for the "Big Event," but it will—I hope—tickle your soon-to-be-wedded funny bone.

The modern wedding, in all its glory and splendor, is a combination of well-intentioned sentiment and pageantry 1990s style. From confetti streamers to skywriters spelling out the couple's names in a giant heart, a wedding is a celebration of love. And it's love that is evident in the eyes of the bride and groom as they look at one another, in the eyes of their parents and families as they take in the ceremony, and in the eyes of the guests as they watch the dessert table being wheeled out.

Weddings are hard work—from planning to honeymooning, there is a lot to talk about. So let's commence to sink our proverbial teeth into some wedding cake and find out what all this planning is really about.

Acknowledgments

I'd like to thank several people who helped bring *The Longest Aisle* to fruition. Many thanks to a great editor, Denise; Amy, for her illustrations; Claudia, Roger, and Phil for fabulous photos; Glen in advance for making this book such a hit; my wife, Carol, for reminding me of what we went through in our own planning stages; and all the people interviewed for the proposal stories, wedding glitches, and other anecdotes and tales of wedding mishaps included within. Thanks to all of you.

And I'd like to dedicate this book to my most joyful inspirations to write, to be funny and to be happy, my children, Rebecca and Eric.

1
Getting Married: What It's All About

♥

Love and Marriage

It's been said they go together like a horse and carriage. However, there have been some variations over the years. For example, in 1966 they went together like a Nehru jacket and love beads. In 1984 they went together like Reagan and the White House, and in the mid-1990s they go together like a PC and a fax modem. But no matter how you describe it, love is still the driving force behind most marriages. And it's that love for one another that keeps you going throughout the arduous task of planning your wedding.

How does one describe love? Poets and other authors have been trying to put it into words for centuries. Valentine's Day has commercialized it, Hallmark has publicized it, and Freud even criticized it, but love endures. And it's that sentiment that'll have a host of people in the wedding business falling in love with your (or your family's) hard-earned cash.

As for the other side of the coin, marriage was invented for several reasons. For one, it gave dating a goal and purpose; for another, it provided something to do with excess rice. Marriage saves on paying two rents, it provides for creativity in thinking up excuses why you got home late or forgot to call, and it proves once and for all that a man and woman can coexist for long periods of time under one roof without having sex.

Marriage has been described as an airplane ride of sorts. It starts off with anticipation, while friends and family hug you at the gate. You taxi for a while, getting to know one another, and then you soar off together into the unknown. There's plenty of turbulence and some bad meals along the way, but you weather the storm. And then, just as when the relatives visit, you're handed a mixed bag of nuts. Some flights have stopovers where you can change planes, just as one changes spouses over the years and takes off again. While you fly, or while you're married, you hope that it goes safely.

But if marriage is like flying, planning the wedding is like packing. How do you get the socks, the pants, the shirts, and the underwear in the suitcase and still have room for the blow dryer? The same way you get the reception site, the caterer, the flowers, the wedding band, and the invitations and still have money left for the honeymoon. Like packing, you'll have to leave a few items out in order to include others. And just as you have to be careful which objects you pack next to each other in the suitcase, you'll have the same problem with your seating plans. You may even have to lean on your suitcase to get it closed, as you might have to lean on the bank to help you pay for the wedding.

But don't simply accept these analogies. Below are some other ideas of what planning a wedding is like from those who've done it:

♀

"It's like a marathon…you train and you train and then you run it and before you know it it's over and all you want to do is collapse."

Anthony from Virginia Beach, Virginia

♀

"It's sort of like cooking a gourmet meal. You have so many things to include and recipes to follow to make it come out just right, and you're cooking for hours, like planning the wedding. Then you gulp the meal down and it's over so fast, like the wedding which comes and goes before you know it."

Didi from Greenwich, Connecticut

♀

"It's like a big exam, you study and study for it for hours and it's over before you realize it. And a lot of the details you were worried about weren't even there."

Carol from New York City

♀

"The whole thing is like sex, the planning is like foreplay, slow and you hope it's leading to something successful. The wedding is like sex, it's the peak of all your hard work. And like sex, if you leave it up to him, it'll be done all wrong."

Denise from Boston, Massachusetts

♀

"It's like those guys you see in the Olympics ski jumping. You keep planning and planning, like they keep practicing and practicing...then you go off the cliff and hope to land on your feet and that everyone likes what you've done. I think our wedding would have gotten a good score by the judges."

James from Lansing, Michigan

No matter how you describe it, planning and pulling off a successful wedding is a major achievement.

♥

The Meaning of Commitment

Here are a few questions you may ask yourself to decide if it's time for you to be "committed." Consider them carefully.

1. Does the word *monogamous* roll off your tongue, or get stuck in your throat?
2. Would a double income help pay your rent, or double your MasterCard bill?
3. Is your company's health plan as good as the one offered by your boyfriend or girlfriend's employer?
4. Would a marriage to a member of the opposite sex help dispel rumors about your sexual preference?
5. Have the relatives of your girlfriend/boyfriend written their last will and testament yet? Can a name still be added?

6. Does the fact that your potential spouse is American-born lessen your fears of having to seek a job back in Peru?

7. Has your long-running personal ad been read by more people than the Bible?

8. Does the word *pregnant* mean anything to you?

9. Is a twelve-piece set of fine china very appealing?

10. Would a wedding get your mother off your case?

♥

The Changing Face of Weddings

Once a most formal occasion, the American wedding has changed with the times. Although formal and traditional is still one approach, the era in which one is getting married does play a part in wedding etiquette and style. For example, in 1968 it wasn't uncommon to see a tie-dyed wedding gown strewn with love beads as the couple walked down the aisle to "In-A-Gadda-Da-Vida." In fact, it wasn't uncommon for the bride and groom to be married not only to each other but to a communal family of twelve (talk about your complicated wedding rehearsals). In 1979 it wasn't uncommon for the bride and groom to be married under a disco ball, and hustle as their first dance to the sounds of *Saturday Night Fever*. Thank goodness that's over!

The reality is that you can always opt for the good old traditional wedding, or you can marry 1990s style in the most trendy fashion of the day.

Below is a comparison of the traditional and trendy wedding styles. Consider both, but don't be surprised if you fall somewhere in between.

Δ

	Traditional	*Trendy*
Proposal:	Romantic setting, he's on one knee.	"Will you marry me?" flashes across the Diamond Vision message board between innings at Mets–Dodgers game.

	Traditional	Trendy
Planning:	Bride's parents plan the wedding.	Bride and groom's lawyers draw up prenuptial agreement.
Bridal Party:	Parents, brothers, sisters, grandparents, and close friends.	Parents, siblings, grandparents, friends, ex-spouses, parent's new spouses or dates, your inner child, etc.
Bridal Shower:	Surprise. Wishing well, practical gifts. Make hat from ribbons and bows.	Surprise. Male stripper, gifts from Victoria's Secret. Make hat from stripper's jock strap.
Customs:	Bride and groom don't see each other on day of wedding until she walks down the aisle.	Bride and groom wake up together and have breakfast and perhaps a "quickie" before heading to the altar.
Processional:	Walk down aisle to "Here Comes the Bride."	Bop down aisle to a ballad by Pearl Jam.
Gown:	Full-length silk or taffeta, lace, beads, pearls, lily-white.	Mini, form-fitting, open back, low-cut front, plenty of accessories, still white.
Ceremony:	Have clergy recite traditional vows in accordance with your religious affiliations.	Write your own vows based on a touching moment from a "Cheers" rerun or a Billy Joel lyric.
Final Declaration:	"I now pronounce you husband and wife."	"I now pronounce you two equal married partners."
Kiss at the altar:	Brief, passionate.	Long, passionate, tongues visible.
First Song:	A romantic tune from a Rodgers and Hammerstein show or one by Gershwin.	Something from Snoop Doggie Dogg or Mariah Carey.
Food:	Prime ribs or chicken as a main course.	Vegetarian, no fat, no additives, lots of herbs, fruits and salads.
Toast:	"May you enjoy many happy years of wedded bliss together and have a large happy family."	"Try to respect each other's space, don't let the sex become monotonous, and have a well-adjusted family."

	Traditional	*Trendy*
Cake:	Five tiers of butter cream, whipped cream, and plenty of sugar.	No sugar, low sodium, low cholesterol, carob; basically no taste.
Honeymoon:	A romantic location and plenty of sex.	An exotic location and plenty of sex.
After the wedding:	He returns to full-time job, she sets up the home.	They both return to busy full-time careers and pencil in when they'll have time to see each other again.
First Anniversary:	They break out the frozen piece of wedding cake and wait until it defrosts to eat it.	They zap a slice of wedding cake in the microwave (a wedding gift) to defrost it.

♥

Famous Marriages Made Just Short of Heaven

TINY TIM AND MISS VICKI *(Married on "The Tonight Show"):*
A marriage made in Burbank. Like so many of those celebrity marriages, it didn't last. But after all, how many times should one person have to endure "Tip-toe Thru' the Tulips"? Talk about cruel and unusual punishment!

♄

PRINCE CHARLES AND LADY DI'S ROYAL WEDDING:
Lavish wedding, but the marriage turned out to be a royal fiasco. Tabloids around the world were the only ones who reaped the benefits of this Cinderella story with a "Nightmare on Barnaby Street" ending.

♄

DONALD TRUMP AND MARLA MAPLES:
Golddigger snags media-hound millionaire. The "money is no object" wedding of the decade was one of "true love," not to mention the couple already being new parents. Naturally, Donald was smart enough this time to make her sign a prenup.

ELVIS AND PRISCILLA PRESLEY:
Many hearts were broken when the king chose a sixth-grader for his bride. Rumor has it that even today, Priscilla, whose acting career has paired her with the equally sexy Leslie Nielsen, occasionally visits Vegas to relive old times with an Elvis impressionist (from the early years, of course).

Δ

JANE FONDA AND TED TURNER:
She's fit, he's rich, and together they do the Atlanta Braves chop. What more could a couple of their great wealth and fame want? Rumor has it that their wedding photographs were taken in black and white so Ted could colorize them.

Δ

BURT REYNOLDS AND LONI ANDERSON:
The one-time *Cosmo* centerfold and WKRP's vivacious receptionist, or "front" lady as some people put it, had a brief marriage and a tabloid-style divorce. Could it have been looks that got these two together? Obviously fidelity, honesty, and trust weren't factored in, but remember, it's Hollywood.

Δ

CHRIS EVERT AND JIMMY CONNORS:
Engaged, they never actually made it to the net together. Too bad, though, we were all anticipating their china pattern—green with white lines. It never happened...one can only assume that "love" meant nothing to them.

Δ

MARILYN MONROE AND JOE DIMAGGIO:
This one goes back a bit, but they were two of America's legends. Once again it makes you wonder, "How come the most beautiful women are seen with such ordinary-looking Joes?"

Δ

LUCILLE BALL & DESI ARNAZ:
Cuban band leader and dizzy redhead...hey, that's a great idea for a television show. Thanks to reruns and worldwide appeal, the show outlasted the marriage.

BRUCE WILLIS AND DEMI MOORE:
His success on the screen has diminished, but not in the bedroom. Look at any newsstand and you're bound to see Demi's big round belly protruding from a magazine cover, ready to produce yet another actor or actress.

♤

ROMEO AND JULIET:
Did themselves in at the thought of having to write thank-you notes.

♤

JOHN MCENROE AND TATUM O'NEAL:
No longer together; one can only wonder how she put up with their arguments.

♤

WOODY ALLEN & MIA FARROW:
Never actually married. Thank goodness, or there might have been more children to fight over.

♤

GEORGE AND MARTHA WASHINGTON:
Had first-ever money fight after historic coin-into-the-river incident.

♤

KIM BASINGER AND ALEC BALDWIN:
Wouldn't you love to be a fly on the bedroom wall when this steamy couple hits the sheets?

♤

KING HENRY VIII AND ANN BOLEYN:
First husband to hoard the remote control. Long before television, it operated an axe.

Wedding Quiz

1. Banging a fork or knife against a drinking glass is a signal meaning:
   A. More champagne
   B. The guests want to see the bride and groom kiss.
   C. A guest is trying to play "Wipe Out" on the crystal.

2. The traditional toast should be done by:
   A. The best man.
   B. A close friend or relative.
   C. Someone who's just completed step four of an Alcoholics Anonymous twelve-step program.

3. When the bride throws the bouquet it means:
   A. The woman who caught it is next to get married.
   B. The woman who caught it gets to sleep with the bandleader.
   C. The person who gets hit in the face by the bouquet can sue both the couple and the florist.

4. The man who catches the garter:
   A. Places it on the leg of the woman who caught the bouquet.
   B. Gets to sleep with the woman who caught the bouquet.
   C. Must wear it himself along with pumps and chiffon.

5. To the back of the wedding vehicle one ties:
   A. Tin cans.
   B. Duplicate gifts.
   C. Ex-lovers.

6. Rice should be thrown:
   A. To symbolize fertility.
   B. At the reception to start a food fight.
   C. With brown gravy on it.

7. A marriage license:
   A. Binds you in wedlock by the state.
   B. Can be revoked by a marriage counselor or a disgruntled relative or an ex-lover.
   C. Is good for only thirty days in California.

8. The top of the wedding cake is traditionally:
   A. Saved and eaten on the first anniversary.
   B. Saved and used as evidence in the divorce trial.
   C. Smeared all over each other on the honeymoon.

9. The ceremony traditionally ends when:
   A. The couple kisses.
   B. Someone objects.
   C. The fat lady sings.
   D. The groom runs from the altar screaming.

10. A white wedding gown symbolizes:
    A. The bride's purity.
    B. The bride's color-blindness.
    C. Mom and Dad's delusion of the bride's purity.

♥

Common Questions and Answers

Below are some actual questions and answers to wedding dilemmas that often arise. Perhaps you'll find the answers to some of your own wedding planning questions below.

Q: My parents are divorced and I hardly ever saw my father. Should he be invited to the wedding?

A: Yes, he should be invited and handed the bill for the occasion, possibly by an attorney, at the end of the affair.

♈

Q: My fiancé doesn't want me inviting my ex-husband to the wedding, but we're still close friends. Should I insist on inviting him?

A: Yes. Explain to your fiancé that you're inviting your ex-husband and that he's also coming on the honeymoon as well. Then, after a short fight, reach a compromise that he can only come to the wedding, which is all you wanted in the first place.

♈

Q: We are inviting a lot of guests and then leaving on a long honeymoon. Rather than writing out each thank-you note by hand, can't I just send store-bought thank-yous?

A: Since no one really cares about thank-you notes anyway, you can save yourself the time and energy by sending a "chain thank-you note" whereby you send out one thank-you note and have the person receiving it send it on to other people who attended the wedding. Threaten them with bad luck if they don't continue the chain.

♀

Q: My parents want to throw us an engagement party in their home. We were hoping to have it in a restaurant. How can I gently sway them to move it to a restaurant?

A: In a nice way—you simply have to make their home unusable for a party. Short of burning it down, you might have someone with a contagious illness move in with them, thus quarantining the place, or you might cause them a severe termite problem or even have the place condemned. But remember, they're your parents, so whatever you do to temporarily ruin their home, do it with a loving spirit.

♀

Q: I have nine friends I really want to be bridesmaids, but my groom can only come up with four ushers, including my brother. What should we do?

A: You can either have the bridesmaids double up and see if a few don't mind wearing a tuxedo and phony mustache, or you can find more ushers. Have you considered your list of ex-lovers? Might your bridesmaids help you out by hitting a good pick-up joint? Would anyone notice if the busboys at the affair donned tuxedos and walked the aisle? There are lots of solutions if you simply need more guys.

♀

Q: My parents are not very wealthy and we're hoping for a big wedding. My wealthy in-laws have offered to foot most of the bill. How can I say yes to their request without offending my parents?

A: Don't tell your parents. Let them think that what they're paying for is what you actually get on the day of the wedding.

So the inexpensive cake they paid for is suddenly twelve tiers high with a waterfall, and the two musicians just happened to bring five friends along with instruments…let them feel that their dollars are really going a long way. If they catch on, however, apologize often and use some of your in-laws' money to buy them a gift, like a cruise.

Q: My parents are divorced and my mother is dating two different men quite steadily. I'd like her to invite one of them to the wedding, but I don't know how to ask her which one she wants to attend with.

A: I think you owe it to your mother to invite both of them. Perhaps the band can play "Torn Between Two Lovers" and they can dance as a threesome.

♀

Q: My fiancé's parents are divorced and remarried. I'd like to include his stepparents in the ceremony.

A: The proper way of handling such a delicate situation is to have the wedding aisle widened considerably so he can walk down with a set of parents on each arm.

♀

Q: I want my grandmother to be part of the processional, but she's ninety-eight and walks at an extremely slow pace. We only have the chapel for an hour and I'm afraid she won't make it down the aisle in time. What do I do?

A: Have two ushers escort her and subtly lift her off her feet and hustle her down the aisle.

♀

Q: I'm engaged to a man who was just released from prison. He wants to invite some of his inmate friends. If they're allowed out for the wedding, where should we seat them, and do we send them invitations as well? How about the armed guards accompanying them?

A: Proper etiquette is to seat the convicts at their own table with the guards. If there are too many, then sprinkle them in with family members who you feel are either ultraconservative or just plain stuffy. You could send just one invitation marked "Dear Chain Gang" or address them individually by prison number. The guards can be individually invited, but ask that they don't bring guests, just firearms.

♀

Q: My mother-in-law-to-be is dreadfully allergic to flowers. Yet I've always dreamed of a backyard wedding full of flowers. What do I do?

A: The only proper and sincere way of handling this delicate situation is to let her blow up like a balloon. It's your wedding!

Q: My fiancé's sisters have been cruel to me since I met them. Yet despite the fact that I hate their guts, my fiancé insists that the two barracudas are to be in the bridal party. What should I do?

A: Pick the ugliest color and style of bridesmaids' gowns that you can come up with to make them wear. Then choose equally unattractive accessories.

♀

Q: I want to have a dais that seats only the bridal party and have their guests and spouses sit at a separate table. My fiancé says that it will ruin the wedding for them and we should have one big table for the bridal party and their guests. What is the proper way to do it?

A: It's very common to have just the bridal party sitting at the dais. Their guests and spouses can sit by themselves at a separate table over in the corner. Remember, the most important thing is that it's your wedding, and it's imperative that it look exactly the way you want it to. It's not important whether anyone other than you has a good time.

♀

Q: My uncle is a Mormon and has six wives. How do we address the invitation?

A: Unless he has a particular wife for attending special occasions, you should invite them all and give them their own special table. They in return should give you a huge gift.

♀

Q: Is there a proper method to numbering the tables at the reception?

A: Yes. People you like most are at table number one, next favorites at table two and so on. Put table one nearest to you and the highest number table in the parking lot.

♀

Q: Is it proper to serve the wedding band a meal?

A: Often they do get a less expensive meal, but if you're looking to save money you might consider inviting them, on their breaks of course, to go from table to table sponging food off the guests' plates.

♀

Q: When a couple is living together, who should pay for their wedding?

A: The parents, since they should be delighted that the couple will no longer be "living together."

Q: One of our dearest friends is a transvestite. Can I ask on the invitation that he come wearing proper attire for a man?

A: No, you must respect what he's all about and allow him to come in drag. You should even consider making him a bridesmaid.

♀

Q: Is it tacky to release a flock of white doves at our outdoor reception?

A: At an outdoor reception, it's not. Just make sure you don't feed them just before releasing them over the heads of your guests.

♀

Q: My cousin and I are getting married in a double wedding. Are there special procedures to follow in a double wedding?

A: Yes, everything must be done in duplicate: two centerpieces, two wedding rings, two cakes, etc. Just be extra careful that when the four of you are standing at the altar the correct bride marries the correct groom.

2
The First Steps

♥

Proposals

You're probably past the proposal stage, but it's always fun to see how your proposal measured up in terms of originality and romantic sentiment. You may have noticed that the manner in which he "pops the question" usually reflects the personalities and careers of those involved. For instance, the thrill seeker might have WILL YOU MARRY ME? spelled out on his parachute, while the more conservative business-man might have his secretary take a letter beginning "Dear so and so, In regard to our current relationship I think some changes might be in order..." The writer may put his feelings on paper, the artist may scroll the proposal across a giant canvas, and the broadcaster may propose over the airwaves, as did Amad Rashad, who proposed to Phylicia on national television.

Since it's usually the man doing the asking, he has usually determined in advance how he's going to do the deed. Will it be the traditional on-one-knee approach? Perhaps sliding naked down the chimney on Christmas with the words WILL YOU MARRY ME tattooed on his butt. There's no set manner anymore, as evidenced by the actual proposals listed below:

❣

Jim, a lifeguard, had the right idea for his beach-loving girlfriend, Janet. He had his proposal on a sign towed behind a small plane flying along the shoreline. "Janet, will you marry me? Jim" brought him nine "yes" responses from various Janets on the beach that day. Happily, one of them was the right Janet.

15

Rick told Carol, while they were visiting a plush Caribbean resort, that she should always check to see what was written on the back of postcards. Not quite understanding the strange suggestion, Carol found out what he meant when one day she returned to their hotel room to find one wall lined with postcards. Turning each one over she read, letter by letter, WILL YOU MARRY ME? Yes, there was a postcard for the question mark.

❦

Jay, a doctor, asked his girlfriend, Carol, also a doctor, if she'd look over a prescription he'd written. Carol took a look and found that the prescription said to take one marriage to Jay for a prescribed lifetime. When she was finished laughing, she accepted and immediately called her folks.

❦

Roger, an ardent hockey fan, had the message flashed on the score-board between periods of a New York Rangers game.

❦

Michael took off his baseball cap to show his girlfriend, Jacklyn, his new haircut. The haircut included two words MARRY ME? shaved into his hair. The style's called a fade, and it must have worked because they've faded into a happy marriage.

❦

Edward took the time and trouble to spray-paint the words on the top of a local video arcade at an amusement park. He then took Cindy on the Ferris wheel where she looked down on the roof and, instead of seeing asphalt, read the romantic proposal.

❦

One clever horse player took his girlfriend to the track and handed her a phony race card for the first race. The number-one horse was called WILL YOU MARRY ME BETTY? She took that bet.

❦

Morris had the waiter at a fine French restaurant bring over the pastry dessert cart. The cake recommended by the waiter had the words WILL YOU MARRY ME? printed on top of it, with a ring nestled in one of the decorative flowers.

Claudia, deciding to take matters into her own hands, had her friends on the college football cheerleading squad spell out her proposal to Frank, who was both surprised and delighted.

❦

Audio technical whiz Gary placed a tiny tape recorder with his proposal inside a large seashell and reminded his girlfriend, Patty, about putting a shell to your ear to hear the sea. Patty quite unsuspectingly heard more than just the sea from that special shell.

❦

Elaine, a schoolteacher, dated a guy who collected valuable rocks and stones. One day she was looking at his collection and noticed a particularly shiny stone. On closer inspection it turned out to be an engagement ring. Said Elaine later of the proposal, "It was a very clever way of proposing. I should have said yes."

❦

Sometimes it's not the question, but the answer that couples remember. Linda and Chris were on a romantic cruise when Chris popped the question. Linda responded with, "I have to check with my therapist first." She did. Her therapist thought it was a terrific idea, and ever since she and Chris have had a marvelous marriage.

❦

It's not just how romantic the proposal is or where it took place, but how it is phrased that makes a proposal memorable in your mind. Beyond the more typical "Will you marry me?" are some variations, such as the ambivalent approach as demonstrated by Andy: "If I were to ask you to marry me, what do you think you'd say?" Penny, now his wife of over fifteen years, responded with, "I don't know, it all depends... was that a proposal?" Then, of course, there's the reasonably pessimistic start to any marriage with the proposal "You don't think we should get married, do you?"

❦

One of the more entertaining proposals in recent memory came from the scriptwriters of television's "Cheers" when coach Ernie Pantuso proposed with a lengthy preamble: "I'm not a rich man, I'm not a strong man, I'm not an educated man, I'm not a tall man, I'm not a gingerbread man, I'm not a milkman..." and on and on he went.

One Final True Proposal Story

Ron, a court reporter now in his mid-thirties, recalls his wife Elizabeth's response. "She told me I had to okay it with her father. So one evening we were at her folks' house and she tells me that he's upstairs by himself and it would be the perfect time to go and talk to him. I remember asking her if he knew anything about this and she told me no, nothing at all. I said are you sure, and again she said don't worry, he doesn't know anything about it. So I went upstairs, knocked on the door to his den and he told me to come in. There, inside the den, he's sitting with two chairs facing him and he asks me where's Elizabeth. I told him that I had something to discuss with him and went on to explain that I wanted to marry his daughter. To this he responds by whipping out a full-page article from the Sunday *Times* on divorce in America and hands it to me asking my opinion on divorce. He then went on to talk about marriage, his daughter, relationships, and so on. Meanwhile, I'm thinking this is pretty good for a guy who didn't know anything about my intentions. The next day, in fact, he called me to tell me he'd booked the hall."

♥

Engagements: A Time to Prepare

The engagement period is the pre-wedding time for preparation. Not only are you planning the wedding itself, but you're also planning your upcoming life together. Below are some of the concerns that will arise. How you answer the following questions is very important to your future together.

✖

Do you want to own or rent your home?

Does the concept of a thirty-year mortgage scare you more than the idea of marriage itself?

Could you get both sets of furniture into a two-room apartment?

Do you want a large apartment for children someday, but with a guest room until then? And exactly who will stay in that guest room? And for how long?

Could you reside in the apartment over your in-laws' garage for more than six months without killing them both in their sleep?

Would a motor home be the best way to spend equal time with both sets of in-laws and pick up and leave town whenever necessary?

Do you want a house furnished in French Provincial while he wants a combination of Early American Howard Johnson's and Modern Disaster Area?

Whose car do you keep?

Do you feel comfortable driving his precious car, even though he winces at the thought of it?

Does he hate your car because he thinks he looks "uncool" driving a beige Nova?

Can you find a studio apartment with a two-car garage?

How about handling money together?

Will you invest your money in IRAs, bonds, and mutuals or dump it into a future oceanside development project in Pennsylvania?

Will you be overdrawn on your joint checking account before you return from the honeymoon?

What about family?

Did he consider the movie *Parenthood* the scariest horror film ever made?

Did the television show "Eight Is Enough" bring tears to your eyes?

Does he want to wait five years before even committing to a house pet, much less children?

Do you hope to be pregnant by the end of the honeymoon?

Would you prefer a career and being called executive vice president much more than "Mommy"?

Does he want a family so badly that he's using mesh condoms?

Do you both wince when you hear a baby cry or are you packing a 10,000 Baby Names book to take on your honeymoon?

What about pets?

Has he threatened to trade your cat in for a foot stand?

Is his dog a little too playful, to the point where you're considering tossing a Frisbee off the edge of the Grand Canyon and yelling "go fetch"?

✗

These are just some of the areas you'll need to discuss, besides planning the wedding itself. Otherwise the engaged couple, that's you, is easy to tell from the dating couple or the married couple. Below are a few ways in which you'll appear obviously engaged.

♢

Dating Couple	Engaged Couple	Married Couple
Feign interest in watching video while sexual activity begins.	Go right from the opening credits into foreplay.	Watch entire film if they both stay awake.
Wear clothes that impress and entice each other.	Wear clothes that are easy to get out of.	Wear whatever's comfortable and doesn't smell.
Fantasize about each other naked.	Act out fantasies	Daydream about new ways to rearrange the living room furniture.
Mild disagreement.	Short fight, long makeup session.	$9,000 at marriage counselor.
Mutual interest	Mutual orgasm	Mutual of Omaha
"We'll pick a show we both want to watch."	"It's okay if you choose the program."	"Gimme the damn remote or I'll break your arm!"
"It's nice to meet you, Mrs. Smith."	"Can I call you Mom?"	"If she stays, I'm leaving."
Conversation about both of your likes and dislikes.	Conversation about the wedding.	What conversation?
Don't notice bad habits.	Notice each other's adorable little habits.	"STOP DOING THAT, IT DRIVES ME UP THE WALL!"

Dating Couple	Engaged Couple	Married Couple
Sit across from each other at restaurant and hang on every word the other says.	Sit next to each other at restaurant and play footsies under the table.	Sit wherever there's leg room and listen to conversations at other tables.
Excited about the relationship.	Excited about the ring.	Excited about new floral pattern on kitchen wallpaper.
Can split up at any time.	Could call the whole thing off.	Could get divorced but like the secure feeling of having someone there who loves and cares about them.

※

♥

Short Versus Long Engagements

Usually a couple is engaged for anywhere from six months to a little over a year. A lot depends on who's going to school, finding a house or apartment, planning the wedding, waiting for the divorce to become final, etc. However, engagements that are relatively long (two or three years) or relatively short (a few weeks or an elopement) say something about the couple.

So what exactly are people saying about you?

Engagements

Very Short	Very Long
She's afraid he'll back out.	He's not ready.
She won't let him until after they're married.	What's the rush, they're living together anyway.
I bet she's pregnant.	They're too wrapped up in their careers.

Very Short	Very Long
They're so in love.	I bet he/she is still playing the field.
This'll kill your father!	How about while your mother and I are still able to attend!
They can't afford a large wedding.	It takes a lot of time to plan a huge, ostentatious affair.
They're impulsive.	They're saving up.
It won't last.	If they make it to the altar, it'll last.
He swept her off her feet!	They've got their feet firmly planted on the ground.
It's so romantic.	The sex probably isn't that good.

♥

Buying the Ring(s)

The engagement ring is more than just an important item of jewelry to be flashed in the faces of all those with whom the bride comes in contact. It is a statement that says a lot about the groom based on its size, luster, and expense. Below is a list of what diamond ring size says.

◇

Ring Size	What Your Ring Is Saying
5 karats or more	I'm marrying Donald Trump!
3 to 5 karats	He's rich, he's mine! Eat your hearts out!
2 to 3 karats	We're your basic yuppies.
1 to 2 karats	We could be yuppies, we're just more conservative with our money.
.75 to 1 karat	He's building a career.
.50 to .75 karat	He's going to be building a career as soon as we get that bank loan.
.25 to .50 karat	Size doesn't matter.

Ring Size	*What Your Ring Is Saying*
Diamond chips	He's really great in bed.
Baguettes	He's a performance artist.
Stone to be determined later.	At least he doesn't have a prison record.

◇

Ring-Buying Tips

1. Shop at a reputable jeweler's...one having those special magnifying glasses known as loupes.

2. Compare prices, but never ask whether the ring is returnable after five to seven years if the marriage hits the skids.

3. Never buy jewelry from a guy selling paintings of James Dean on velvet from the sidewalk.

4. Spend approximately: five weeks' salary, nine unemployment checks, 16 percent of what your rich uncle left you, or everything in your piggy bank.

5. No respectable jeweler operates from the back of a Toyota hatchback.

6. Don't let the jeweler talk you into mortgaging your new home to pay for the ring.

7. Get a written appraisal by someone other than the jeweler's assistant who repairs watches on a work release program from the state penitentiary.

8. Also get an appraisal from a local pawnshop, just in case.

9. Don't buy an engagement ring off the Home Shopping Club.

10. Be careful never to get a ring that's well out of your price range stuck on your finger.

11. Don't postpone a wedding until a relative with a "major stone" keels over in hopes of getting it in the inheritance.

12. Never put up your fiancé as collateral.

13. Try not to put up your mother-in-law as collateral.

14. If it can't cut through a napkin, it's not a diamond.

◇

Ring-Shopping Guidelines

1. Set a price range somewhere between what the groom-to-be spends on his wardrobe in a year and what Whoopi Goldberg was paid to appear in *Sister Act II* ($7 million).

2. Ask around for a good jeweler—one who never uses the term "retail price" unless it's a comparison to his own price.

3. Have the jeweler show you every ring in the store, even high school graduation rings. But don't buy anything without looking at every ring in another store.

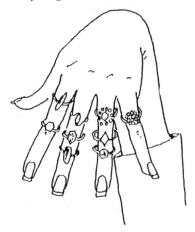

4. Wave the rings in other customers' faces. Reaction to your ring is important.

5. Ask questions about Tiffany settings, channel settings, table settings, and other diamond-related terms to appear intelligent.

6. Don't include the jeweler in your personal arguments.

7. Make sure the jeweler knows that you're going to have the ring appraised the minute you leave the store by one of the foremost gem experts in the country, and if he or she doesn't agree with the value of the ring, you will not only return the ring, but will bring a television news crew to expose "the crooked jeweler."

The Four C's

Diamond retailers stress the four C's when buying a diamond.

◇

First is the *cut* of the stone, or its shape. Diamonds can be round, oval, pear-shaped, or cut to look like the head of a former head of state. The cut is important because it results in that proper glaring sparkle that you want reflecting into the eyes of your friends and relatives.

◇

The Test: A good way to test the cut is to stand along a beach on a sunny day and see if, by holding your arm and ring outstretched at a 45° angle toward the sky, you can momentarily blind an elderly couple playing shuffleboard on a passing cruise ship.

◇

Clarity is the next of the four C's. Clarity defines how perfect the diamond is inside. Many diamonds contain some minor imperfections noticeable only to the eye of a well-trained jeweler or perhaps Elizabeth Taylor or Zsa Zsa Gabor. If your diamond is flawless, it is valuable and you should carry a magnifying glass with you at all times to hand to friends and relatives.

◇

The Test: Sterilize a needle and then prick yourself in the finger. Next, stain a microscope slide with your own blood. Look through a microscope to be sure you find at least one blood cell. Wait until the blood dries and then place the diamond over the slide. If you can still see that blood cell at all times, even when moving the diamond around, and nothing is blocking or distorting your view, then there is no imperfection in that stone, except perhaps for some dried blood on it.

◇

The third C is *color*. A diamond should ideally be colorless, allowing light to reflect from it. Thus, if someone tells you an orange diamond is valuable, he's lying.

◇

The Test: Buy a hundred cans of different colored paint. Spread a dab of each color on a flawless, pure white canvas. Place a large piece of pure white paper on the floor in front of the canvas. Stand completely naked in front of the canvas (clothes could reflect unwanted colors) and have someone (preferably someone you know well) stand on a ladder and reflect a flashlight at a 45° angle at the ring, which you hold 2.5 inches in front of each color. The ring should reflect that color clearly onto the paper below. Any color that isn't crystal clear is being altered by a color in your ring. The more clear colors that are reflected, the more colorless your ring must be.

◇

The final C is *cost*. Your ring should cost more than anything your fiancé has bought either you or himself since you two have known each other. The cost should reflect his love for you and willingness to forgo a much-needed new transmission and his membership at the local gym.

◇

The Test: Have the jeweler show your fiancé three rings of varying cost. Tell the jeweler that the middle one is the one you really like. (Don't say the one you "want," only the one you "seem to like.") Next have a friend call your fiancé, just before he leaves for the jeweler and offer to sell him Super Bowl tickets. If he bypasses the tickets and buys you the most expensive of the three rings, you've established that your ring represents his love and willingness to sacrifice and also costs a hell of a lot of money.

♥

Engagement Parties

The engagement party is the perfect time to show off the engagement ring to friends and family at one time. It is also a good way to determine whom you should and shouldn't include in your wedding party and who should sit with whom at the ceremony. In fact, you may even decide not to invite certain guests to "the main event" based on their showing or lack of showing at your engagement party. In short, it's a way to celebrate the fact that he finally popped the question, while at the same time receiving gifts and auditioning your prospective wedding guests.

Watch your guests carefully…even videotape the event, not so much for prosterity, but to look for the important details. Note who gave you which gift. Who got drunk and acted inappropriately? Who showed up late? Who dressed in embarrassingly poor taste? Remember, you're scouting to decide who will sit by the dance floor and who will huddle by the kitchen. You're looking to see whom you might choose for special duties and whom you might not remain in contact with during the ten or twelve months leading up to the big day.

The engagement party should have a warm, homey feel to it, be it a restaurant affair or in someone's house. If the engagement party rivals the wedding in scope and grandeur the wedding will seem anticlimactic. One groom noted that when the band and two hundred guests sang "The Bride Cuts the Cake" (as they stood by their five-tier engagement party cake, complete with miniature bride and groom), he began to wonder if they were already married.

Engagement parties are also a nice time to see how well your families mingle. Often they haven't had much of a chance, if any, to spend time together. Listen for clues and indications so you'll know how well they're getting along. Phrases like "I'm sure we'll be seeing a lot of each other" and "We'll have to have you over for dinner" are a good sign. Phrases such as "This party could have been done so much better," "What kind of people are you?" or "I've seen servants' quarters that look better than this" are definite signs that the families are not ready to coexist in harmony and peace.

Besides auditioning family and friends and hoping that future in-laws don't become feuding outlaws, you should spend a portion of the festivities opening your engagement presents. The trick is to see how utterly thrilled you can act when opening the same cake-serving dish five times. It's also important that you show the same exuberance for a $12 aluminum napkin holder as you show for a $500 piece of fine crystal. You might consider taking a couple of acting lessons, or you might use those skills you've built up over the years. For example, ladies, you may recall the last time you faked it, and, gentlemen, you might remember the last time you told a woman "I'll call you." These skills come in handy when opening gifts before a roomful of people.

♥

Scheduling the Big Event

The scheduling of the wedding is the first step on the long road of preparations. It is an important decision that takes numerous factors into account. Below are some of the responses you'll hear when choosing potential dates for the wedding.

"It might snow."

"That's hurricane season."

"The airfares are too expensive."

"It's too near Christmas."

"Your father and I are going to Europe that Wednesday."

"Your cousin Sheila's getting married the following Sunday."

"Isn't that Passover?"

"It's Super Bowl Sunday, forget it."

"Your brother leaves for school that week."

"Your brother won't be back from school yet."

"Nobody gets married on the thirteenth."

"That's Easter Sunday."

"Too near Thanksgiving."

"It's a full moon, that's not good."

"The minister plays golf that day."

"It's your nephew's first birthday party."

"It's too close to Sheldon's bar mitzvah."

"That's the week your great-aunt Selma spends at the yoga retreat in Norway."

"Too near Presidents' Day."

"Doesn't your aunt Zelda fast on Sundays?"

"Your cousin Phil doesn't get paroled until the following Wednesday."

"The Schlboykins are religious, they won't come that day."

"Isn't that the day Halley's Commet will be visible?"

"That's the week Annie [your matron of honor] is due to have the
   baby."

"My psychic said that's not a good time for a wedding."

"Not during tax season!"

"That's the day of my Fantasy Baseball League draft."

And then there are your own personal considerations and reasons
why a particular date just isn't right for one of you.

"That'll be my time of the month."

"The playoffs start that week."

"That's the week I'm getting my job evaluation."

"Isn't that the day Elvis died?"

And then there are the considerations of the clergy and reasons
why a particular date may not be right, whatever your religion may be.

"It's a holy day, I'm not sure why, but it is."

"Sorry, it's our bingo night."

"Can't do, religious retreat."

And then there are considerations of the place in which you wish
to hold the blessed event.

"Sorry, we've got the Sons of Satan Tennis Tourney that weekend."

"That's the week the exterminator will be spraying the place."

"Our staff is threatening a wildcat strike that weekend."

"Only if you want to share the day with the Sheepherders of
   America...it's their annual barn dance and picnic."

"We're in Chapter 11 and who knows if we'll still be here
by then."

When you finally do select the date and it sits well with the
immediate family, go to the printer and order invitations before anyone
can come up with a last-second reason for you to change it.

♥

The Wedding Calendar

Yes, grooms are more involved these days in the wedding plans—and why not, in this economy they (and the bride) are usually paying for at least one third of the cost of the wedding. Here is the traditional timetable for the wedding from the bride's and the groom's standpoints.

The Bride	*The Groom*
9–12 Months Before Wedding	
Start planning the reception and budget out wedding costs.	Hock possessions to pay for engagement ring.
6–9 Months Before Wedding	
Decide on details such as flowers, decor, and photographer. Order your dress and decide on dresses for bridal party.	Enter office football pool or start planning for rotisserie league draft. Plan ski trip with friends. Join bowling league.
3–6 Months Before Wedding	
Finish guest list. Go for fittings on gown. Arrange for time off for honeymoon.	Remember to tell a few friends and your parents you're getting married.
8 Weeks Before Wedding	
Mail invitations. Choose gifts for bridal party. Confirm with photographer, band, etc.	Nudge best man to plan bachelor party. Debate final fling with office temp or old girlfriend.
2 Weeks Before Wedding	
Drag groom along to get license. Check honeymoon reservations. Complete last hundred or so little details.	Inform softball team that you might miss a couple of games. Put in request for vacation time.

One Week Before Wedding

Be surprised by X-rated lingerie at the bridal shower.

Be surprised by X-rated guest at bachelor party.

Final Days Before Wedding

Sit back and anticipate the big day. Reminisce with friends and family. Start thinking about future home and family.

PANIC! Get tuxedo, pick up wedding ring, get a passport, find some clean clothes for honeymoon. Surreptitiously find out from someone in bridal party where the reception will be held. Anticipate big day with dread and fear.

♥

The High Cost of Putting It All Together: Who Pays?

In today's economy it is not uncommon for the bride and groom's families, and even the bride and groom themselves, to work together in footing the bill for a wedding. And since weddings commonly run in the $12,000-to-$20,000 range, it's not uncommon for those footing the bill to have high blood pressure by the time the big event is ready to commence.

There are ways to cut corners and keep some of the costs down, but no matter how you arrange it, a full-scale wedding is a costly undertaking. Below are just a few of the expenses you can expect to incur along the way.

- Bridal attire, including gown, veil, shoes, gloves, stockings, garter, underwear, last-minute alterations, sash, scarf, contact lenses, backup pair of contact lenses, dress, coat and shoes for rehearsal dinners, engagement party dress, and complete ensemble for honeymoon

- Groom's attire: tuxedo for day of wedding—rented
- Reception costs, including food, beverages, service, room rental, tips, and payment for whatever your uncle breaks trying to prove he can still do the old tablecloth trick after five glasses of champagne

And let's not forget the other elements that no full-fledged wedding can be without:

- The photographer, video guy, flowers, the band, limousines, invitations, thank-you notes, place cards, calligrapher, centerpieces, rice, tin cans, cake, figurines, clergy's fee, tarot card reader, gifts for attendants, gifts for the guests, gifts for valet parking attendants, gifts for passersby during the ceremony, jugglers, mimes, roving magicians, ice sculptures of Donald Trump and Marla, a waterfall or stream, hot air balloonists, a marching band, a flock of doves, the Boston Symphony, a squadron of air force fighters flying in formation, and the entire Broadway cast of *Les Misérables*.

And these are just a few of the essentials!

Once the essentials are established, any top-notch catering facility or wedding planner will ask you if you'd like to add those little "extras" aimed at impressing your guests. But this is the time to ask yourself if you really need these items to make your wedding special:

🍽️

Do you really need Tom Jones in person to sing "What's New, Pussycat"?

Isn't a thirty-nine-layer cake a little excessive? (Especially since the plastic figures are up so high that they're getting nosebleeds.)

Do you really need chinchilla tablecloths?

Aren't authentic Ming vases just a tad ostentatious for centerpieces?

Valet parking is nice, but having the fellows wash and polish each and every car may be excessive.

Isn't a sit-down meal for 200 a bit much for the rehearsal dinner?

Must the catering hall charge you extra to fly in each imported cheese from its country of origin?

Hiring a limo is common, but buying one just for the wedding might be a bit extravagant.

♥

Money-Saving Tips

The modern wedding is an expensive proposition. Therefore, it's always a good idea to cut corners wherever possible. Below are twenty money-saving tips that every bride and groom should keep in mind for the big event.

1. Weekday weddings are cheaper. What guest won't welcome a day off from work to attend your Monday afternoon reception?

2. Finger foods are less expensive. For that matter, you could try the new McWedding hors d'oeuvres.

3. Picking flowers from neighbors' yards is an easy and inexpensive way to create your bouquet.

4. Hang out at a local hospital and "borrow" flowers from rooms when patients are sleeping.

5. Domestic wines are cheaper than imported. Bartles & Jaymes is even cheaper.

6. Hamburger Helper can make your main course go a long way.

7. Check out relatives' closets and attics. Find a wedding dress you like, then tell its owner how much you wish you could find a dress just like hers. If she doesn't get the hint, steal it.

8. Pick up thrown rice and boil it to be served as a side dish.

9. Put guests up with friends or family or at the local Y.

10. If you must put guests up at a hotel, double them up. And remember Motel 6.

11. Have your bridal party cram into a photo booth at Woolworth's for inexpensive pictures.

12. Doggie bags! If you've paid for of 150 dinners and only 100 people show up, that's 50 free meals for you to take on your honeymoon.

13. Honeymoon in Cleveland. If you intend to spend the entire time in bed, why waste money on an exotic location?

14. Sixteen Sara Lee cakes smashed together and covered with frosting look just like any other wedding cake. And probably taste just as good if not better.

15. Hire three local street musicians with kazoos who know how to play the "Wedding March."

16. Drive slowly so as not to damage cans tied to the bumper, then untie them and return them for the deposits.

17. Plan off-season honeymoon destinations, like Florida during hurricane season or ski country in early August.

18. Pack the entire bridal party into one stretch limousine.

19. Make your wedding invitations an assignment for a local fifth-grade arts and crafts class.

20. Buy fabric at a Presidents' Day white sale and make your own wedding gown. Use whatever is left over for napkins.

♥

The Wedding Expert

Trying to plan the big event is often a major headache in the scheme of one's daily routine. Therefore, one can rest assured that someone else has thought to profit from your nuptials by becoming a wedding planner. Yes, there are people out there who will take the personal touch from your wedding and turn it into another business transaction. And why not? There's money involved.

In defense of wedding planners, like interior decorators they often know how to get things done quickly, and even get good prices in some areas. But all wedding consultants are not alike. How do you find a good one? How do you know that they'll arrange the wedding you want and not a backyard tent affair when you were partial to an indoor gathering at a catering hall, or vice versa?

Below are some questions to consider when looking for a wedding consultant.

✷ How have her previous weddings worked out? At her last affair were nine people rushed to the hospital with food poisoning?

✷ How often has she had a tent collapse during the ceremony? More than twice is not a good sign.

✷ Do you and the wedding consultant get along? Does the wedding consultant frequently use the phrase "Shut up and listen to me"?

✷ If you want linen and she prefers lace, does she throw a tantrum?

✷ Has the consultant put a wedding-planning gag order on your mother? Mother-in-law? (This may be a good thing.)

✷ What details does she and doesn't she handle? Will you find out two days before the wedding that everything is all set except for the food?

✷ When it comes to decorating the room, will you find out that she doesn't do windows...or centerpieces for that matter?

✷ Does she have an obsessive love of ice sculptures?

✷ How does she get paid for her services? Is it $2,000 in advance so she can skip town to Brazil well before the big event?

✷ Does she get a commission from all the wedding costs, so that she finds you the most expensive florist and caterer in the country?

✖ Does she receive royalty checks every time you successfully pass another wedding anniversary? On the arrival of your firstborn?

✖ Can the planner provide you with references? Do these references use the word *fiasco* in talking about their wedding day? Are they happy to hear from you because they really want to know the whereabouts of the planner?

It's important to know what you're getting into when you let such an important job out of your hands. Often, a friend or family member will offer to do the whole thing for you. This is a big mistake. No matter how well someone thinks she knows you, she's wrong…even your mom. Especially your mom.

Problems You May Run Into When a Friend or Family Member Plans Your Wedding

1. You don't agree on balloon animals for centerpieces at a formal affair.
2. She ends up marrying the groom.
3. She insists on singing a version of "Tomorrow" with the wedding band.
4. The wedding is planned around her schedule, and since she travels on weekends, you're getting married on a Tuesday.
5. Your taste is "modern" and hers is "archaic."
6. She forgets to invite your parents.
7. She schedules it in St. Mary's Cathedral and you and your fiancé are both Jewish.
8. You're deathly allergic to what she's chosen for your bouquet.
9. The choice of a main course is steak or chicken. You're both vegetarians.
10. Your mom plans it and invites a different groom…of her own choosing.

♥

Bridal Magazines

There are several bridal magazines that you'll find in the stores offering the same advice on a quarterly basis. These magazines generally weigh in at about twenty-five-pounds each, so buy them one at time.

Your objective when looking through these magazines is to look at and even rip out the multitude of photos of wedding gowns and accessories, trying to select the look that's right for you. You then browse through the handful of helpful how-to articles but avoid the tips about love and romance, written by some expert whose idea of the ideal man is one who's impressed by a woman who sets a good table.

One should also remember when seeking advice that most bridal magazines' top editors are Amy Vanderbilt clones who think wearing open-toed sandals is a walk on the wild side.

You may look for and find everything you'll need for the wedding in one of these magazines. Now, if only you could afford all of it!

A final note: If the groom even attempts to look at a bridal magazine it can cause temporary blindness, so don't even bother trying to get him interested.

♥

Eight Different Ways to Wed

There is no longer a "standard" or traditional wedding. Today, there are so many choices that include unique themes which can and will enhance your big day. As you plan ahead, consider some of these wedding ideas.

♀ ♂

A Military Wedding: Includes the traditional arch of swords. Groom and ushers wear full military uniforms. Brother of the bride isn't asked and doesn't tell. Best man and ushers are court-martialed for lewd conduct regarding the bridesmaids. A hearing follows.

A Mansion Marriage: Fashion and decor represent the 1890s but prices reflect the 1990s. Bride wears antique gown. Antique cars carry guests, who are stopped at the gate and searched for missing pieces of fine china and priceless crystal.

Wedding at Sea: Marry on a sailing ship while guests not only cry but gag at the railing. Watch overeager guests and bridesmaids chase bouquet into icy waters as bride overthrows her attendants. As your traditional first song ask the band to play "Splish Splash" or the theme from *The Poseidon Adventure.*

Vegas Wedding: The perfect sentimental "quickie" wedding for those who are fed up with their parents' plans to invite just five hundred of your closest friends. Pick a number, then wait your turn to descend down the aisle of matrimony with five gorgeous chorus girls while the Elvis impersonator croons "Love Me Tender" against a backdrop that includes a twenty-nine-foot flashing neon heart.

A Giant Tent Affair: Wed in the great outdoors in a park, large backyard, or toxic-waste site. Include a barbecue to provide plenty of soot for expensive dresses and wedding gown. Use the lovely no-pest strip centerpieces, and if it's a hot day, get to the cake as early as possible. And make sure no one has set the lawn sprinklers on a timer.

Nudist Wedding: This no-holds-barred au naturel way to wed is for the more daring. Bypass long hours of fittings and color-coordinating the dresses. Find out if the best man really is the "best man." Bring plenty of sun block and discover new and inventive places to put gift envelopes.

Surprise Wedding: Invite guests to a party, but don't tell them it's a wedding until they arrive. Have paramedics on hand for astonished in-laws and remember to use the phrase "You can always send us a gift by mail" as often as possible.

Medieval Wedding: The perfect theme for the families that don't get along. Wedding party wears proper period attire, food is devoured without utensils, and jousting and human catapulting is encouraged between families. Expect goats and oxen as gifts; in fact, you might register at the local petting zoo.

♥

Customs

Oh, the modern wedding! It's the 1990s and customs and traditions are changing all the time. Below we've listed some of the traditional ethnic customs for various wedding ceremonies. We've also added the new versions of these older customs for those who want to capture tradition and trendiness in one celebration.

Traditional and Modern Customs

AFRICAN: *TRADITIONAL:* A ceremonial hand washing is used to wash away evil spirits and memories of past lovers.
              MODERN: More than just the hands are washed to forget past lovers.

AMISH:	*TRADITIONAL:* The bride wears new but ordinary clothing, the ceremony is held mid-week and the couple arrives by horse and carriage. *MODERN:* The bride wears new but ordinary clothing, the ceremony is held mid-week, and the couple arrives by horse and carriage.
CARIBBEAN:	*TRADITIONAL:* Couple plants a tree for prosperity. *MODERN:* Couple buys a time share.
CHINESE:	*TRADITIONAL:* Firecrackers are set off. *MODERN:* Firecrackers are sold to the kids in the neighborhood.
FRENCH:	*TRADITIONAL:* The bride buys a new wardrobe for the honeymoon and the wedding is done all in white—decor, gowns, wine, tuxedos, etc. *MODERN:* The bride is given unlimited credit at the department store of her choice and the groom turns white when he sees how much she's spent.
IRISH:	*TRADITIONAL:* Guests throw flower petals at the couple for good luck. *MODERN:* Guests, being environmentally correct, throw paper flower petals, then recycle them.
ITALIAN:	*TRADITIONAL:* The couple has a beautiful, hand-designed busta, or wedding bag, in which to put gifts of money. *MODERN:* The couple has a beautiful, hand-crafted, high-security padlocked safe with a guard in which to put gifts of money.
JAPANESE:	*TRADITIONAL:* Colored candies in the shapes of flowers. *MODERN:* Colored candies in the shapes of electronic equipment.
JEWISH:	*TRADITIONAL:* The groom breaks a glass under his foot to end the ceremony. *MODERN:* The bride makes the groom clean up the broken glass to show who's really in charge.

LATIN AMERICAN:*TRADITIONAL:* The flower girl and ring bearer are dressed as miniature versions of the bride and groom.
MODERN: They're also required to stand on top of the wedding cake.

MEXICAN: *TRADITIONAL:* The groom presents thirteen gold coins to the bride to show he will support her.
MODERN: The groom also presents his last three paychecks and a deed for property in Cancún.

POLISH: *TRADITIONAL:* Children put ropes and chains in the way of the couple's exit. The best man pays them off with candy so the couple can get through.
MODERN: The kids hold the couple ransom for a Nintendo.

PUERTO RICAN: *TRADITIONAL:* Money is pinned to the dress of the bride.
MODERN: Due to the economy, IOU's are pinned instead.

RUSSIAN: *TRADITIONAL:* The couple ties a doll or a bear to the back of their car to indicate whether they want a boy or a girl as their first child.
MODERN: The couple ties a Boris Yeltsin doll to the back of the car to indicate their political preference.

SCANDINAVIAN: *TRADITIONAL:* The bride wears a crown covered with jewels to indicate innocence.
MODERN: The bride adds condoms to the crown to indicate not complete innocence but at least safe sex.

Combining Ethnic Backgrounds

Today, it's not uncommon to find that the bride and groom are of different ethnic backgrounds. Below are some of the traditions that have resulted from such actual ethnic pairings.

A Jewish man married an African woman: The horah was played on a conga drum and the customary wine poured on the ground (African offering to the gods) was Manischewitz. The gods were amused.

An English gentleman married an Amish woman: They rode to the ceremony in a horse and carriage on the wrong side of the road.

A Greek and Mexican couple: They served an intriguing mix of burritos and enchiladas stuffed with feta cheese and grape leaves.

A Scottish man married a Japanese woman: She wore a ceremonial kimono and he wore a traditional kilt. Guests of other ethnic backgrounds kept looking around trying to find the bride and groom.

A Jewish woman married a man from Hawaii: They had a Hawaiian luau, except that instead of a pig they stuck the apple in a giant chopped liver.

Throwing the Bouquet

Throwing the bouquet is a tradition that dates back to ancient times when the idea was to marry off an entire European village by a wedding relay. The bride would toss the bouquet and the woman who caught it would marry almost immediately, then toss the bouquet to the next very-soon-to-be bride. The village that married off the most

brides by this "relay" wedding system was given great prizes and honors by the government, a government that at the time obviously had little else to do and no television game shows to watch.

Today, the throwing of the bouquet symbolizes that the bride wishes the same good nuptial fortune on one of her "unsuspecting" guests.

It's important that the bride get a handle on the proper manner of throwing the bouquet. At some weddings, the chandelier is the lucky recipient of the bridal bouquet. And it is never easy for the guy who catches the garter to slip it onto an ornate, and somewhat hot, chandelier.

Ideally, the toss is an over-the-shoulder reverse-style shotput toss, popular in ancient Greece during the early bridal Olympics. The trick is to hoist it just high and far enough to clear the first two rows of eager bridal wannabes and reach the unsuspecting back row filled with those embarrassingly coaxed and cajoled by other guests to stand there in a shameless display of "still being single at their ages."

It's also important to choose the right kind of bouquet, one that looks stunning when carried down the aisle but is easily transformed into a projectile. The beautiful new floral football display has become increasingly popular with sports-minded brides. Sometimes, brides-to-be are seen in neighborhood parks tossing around the old bouquet in preparation for the big event. Practice, practice, practice.

Tossing the Garter

The garter is similarly tossed at weddings, as a line of eligible bachelors and boys not old enough to have had their skin clear up jockey for position.

Since the male species is immediately drawn into the "foul ball" state of mind, one should remember never to stand too close, as this group will dive in and pile up to catch said garter. Those who know the garter ritual will make a more concerted effort if the catcher of the bouquet is thought to be especially attractive.

The Garter and the Leg Game

The custom of putting the garter onto the leg of the woman who caught the bouquet was established at the wedding of two crew members of the television game show "Let's Make A Deal."

The idea here is to have the lady sit in a chair while the gentleman slides the garter up her leg until she either slaps him in the face or dies of embarrassment. Ideally, the best scenarios are brought about when one of the two participants is the painfully shy "doesn't date much" type, while the other once frequented New York's well-known swingers club Plato's Retreat.

Otherwise, this ritual is solely designed to give the long-married, slightly intoxicated husbands at the affair a momentary vicarious thrill.

3
The Big Steps

♥

Reception Sites

Consider the following factors when choosing a reception site.

🏰

1. *Size*

   Don't trust caterers who assure you they can hold 250 people while a sign on the wall says "Occupancy by more than 125 is dangerous and unlawful."

   If you and your fiancé alone crowd the dance floor, it might not be big enough for 150…either that or you both need a diet.

2. *Privacy*

   Do you really want a country club where golfers are asking the band to stop playing so they can tee off, and where "Simon says" is coming over the public address system?

   Is a backyard wedding a good idea when your next-door neighbors sunbathe nude in their backyard and blast Janet Jackson CDs?

   Do you really want to be taking your vows in a church where you can hear someone in a neighboring room yell out "BINGO!"

3. *Weather*

   Is December really a good time for an outdoor wedding on the shore of one of the Great Lakes?

Summer in Arizona? Outdoors? Afternoon? Not unless you're planning to hold it in a swimming pool.

4. *Season*

Aren't most people busy the week before Christmas?

Does an outdoor reception in hay fever season mean you'll be sneezing your vows?

5. *Accommodations*

Isn't 200 people to one bathroom a bad ratio?

Consider a catering hall too small if the staff can't get your wedding cake inside without dismantling and reassembling it.

By parking available, do the caterers mean their own parking lot or do they mean feeding meters every hour in front of the nearby supermarket?

By "their own catering" do they mean a kitchen and well-planned assortment of foods or are they going to pass around the menu to a Chinese take-out and go pick it up for you?

Avoid an outdoor wedding on any site with sprinklers set on a timer—even if they assure you they'll shut them off.

Has the woman in the coat-check room just been released from a correctional facility for stealing?

♥

The Caterer

Meeting with the caterers is a unique opportunity to hear foods described and offered like trading cards. "We can do a potato salad and cole slaw if you'd prefer instead of the cocktail franks" is a line you'll never hear from anyone other than a caterer. But how do you know what to get? Caterers will try and sell you on everything that they can possibly make (or that they can give you, as they put it—for a price of course). Their plans are carefully designed to be just a little less food than you'll actually need, causing you to order a few "extras" at a higher cost. But it's okay because of the throw-ins. "Take the fruit cup and I'll throw in relish trays with the main course." Who else but a caterer can make you that offer?

The toughest part isn't the main course. Usually you give people a choice of fish, chicken, or red meat (for those who don't want a healthy meal if they're not paying for it). The difficulties lie in the other courses. For example, at some point you may be asked to choose between a garden salad, Caesar salad, chef salad, hearts-of-lettuce salad, cucumber salad, tossed salad, health salad, California salad, green salad, avocado salad, Greek salad, and antipasto, or perhaps stuffed mushrooms instead of a salad. This is what you'll be discussing at GREAT LENGTH with your caterer. And that's not to mention 173 kinds of salad dressings, ranging from Creamy Italian to some blend of Miracle Whip and maple syrup that the caterer calls the "House Specialty Dressing."

NOTE: A good caterer should let you sample some of his food, so show up hungry, holding a knife and fork. If he doesn't get the hint, choose another caterer.

What to Look For in a Good Caterer

1. A good caterer does not have boxes of Shake 'N Bake all over the kitchen.
2. If every time you visit there's an ambulance parked in front of the catering hall, this is not a good sign.
3. A good caterer should know that a kosher meal is not a ham on rye with Swiss.

4. Never trust a "catering facility" that has a giant yellow chicken on the roof.

5. If the caterer thinks a "vegetarian" is someone who doctors sick animals, you're using the wrong person.

6. If the caterer spends more time discussing the ice sculpture than the entrée, find another caterer.

7. Don't trust a caterer who tries to water down Swedish meatballs.

8. If you require a carving knife to cut the chopped liver, this caterer isn't for you.

9. Never trust a caterer who considers Jell-o a green vegetable.

10. No, Pop Tarts are not considered chic hors d'oeuvres.

♥

Whom You Should and Shouldn't Have in Your Bridal Party

Choosing a bridal party can be difficult. Along with appropriate family members, you will want to choose friends and other relatives to walk down the aisle on your big day. These are those special friends or relatives whom you not only want to honor, but who you feel owe you bigger gifts and significant amounts of their time for rehearsals and fittings. These are the people you forever want to look at in 1,200 wedding-day photos and on your wedding video…so choose them wisely.

Below are some simple guidelines you may want to follow when selecting your bridal party.

1. Never choose anyone who is wider than the aisle he will have to walk down.

2. Avoid anyone you suspect has slept with your future spouse.

3. Choose people who will start drinking *after* the ceremony.

4. Retract the invitation from anyone who responds with "Can I get back to you on that in a few weeks?"

5. Avoid asking both parties of a recently divorced couple.

Get to know the groom's closest friends, also known as your ushers.

6. Don't ask a friend in her ninth month to be a bridesmaid.
7. Don't ask a guy who can't even commit to getting cable television to be your best man.
8. Try not to ask anyone who frequents a pawnshop more than twice a year to be the best man and carry the ring.
9. Don't expect anyone who's wanted in six states to walk down the aisle.
10. Ask people who believe in wearing deodorant.

Attendants' Duties

Besides the momentous walk down the aisle, the members of the bridal party have other specific duties they are expected to perform prior to and on the day of the wedding. Let's look at what's expected of each member of your bridal party.

Matron/Maid of Honor

♂

The difference between a matron of honor and a maid of honor is that the matron is married and has the added responsibility of hounding the bride-to-be with endless stories of her wedding and how she planned everything. The maid of honor, on the other hand, has to preface her remarks by repeatedly saying, "When I get married…"

The MOH must also plan the bridal shower. A simple task, the bridal shower must be a complete surprise, inconvenient to no one, at an easy-to-find location, and on the day that the bride-to-be's great-aunt or some such family icon can attend. To accomplish this, the MOH must make numerous job-jeopardizing personal phone calls to a host of the bride-to-be's friends and family members, many of whom she's gone to great lengths at previous social gatherings to avoid. She must not only talk with these people repeatedly, but find them rides.

On the big day, the MOH must help push, squeeze, compress, or do whatever it takes to fit the bride into the gown. The MOH is also given the responsibilities of bridal-room bouncer and moral priestess, keeping all unwanted relatives at bay until after the ceremony and making sure that ushers and bridesmaids avoid getting sauced, high, or intimate until after they've walked down the aisle. The MOH should also help the bride pack for her honeymoon, which these days means bringing the Reddi Wip, condoms, something from the Victoria's Secret catalog, and perhaps a hand puppet.

Immediately following the ceremony it is her job to stand next to the groom in the receiving line and kick him whenever he says something utterly embarrassing to a guest from the bride's side. During the reception, the MOH usually is asked to dance with the best man. Beyond that, she should then be able to drink the five or six tedious months of planning into oblivion.

The Bridesmaids

♂

A bridesmaid's chief function is to hold her head up proudly as she parades through a room filled with 50 to 500 invited guests, wearing the same hideous, butt-magnifying gown as five to ten other women.

Bridesmaids are also required to attend numerous fittings that are designed solely to interfere with their social calendars. They must remain the same weight, shape, and build until after the big event, which means if silicone implants or a breast reduction is forthcoming, don't be a bridesmaid. Breakups that lead to eating binges are also ill-advised.

Other duties of the bridesmaid include:

- Warding off unwanted advances of ushers while flirting with members of the wedding band
- Dancing with the bride's ninety-three-year-old uncle and periodically lifting his hand from her derriere
- Making snide, sarcastic, or disparaging remarks to the other bridesmaids regarding the choice of attire of various female wedding guests, including the groom's mother, his great-aunt, and especially his sister

The Best Man
♀

The most important duties of the best man are to throw the groom one hell of a bachelor party and to be sure he makes it to the ceremony sober and on time. To do this, the best man must possess that special knack for knowing directions to the hottest strip joints in a twenty-mile radius so that he can thoroughly plan an evening of debauchery rivaled only by those of the Kennedy youth.

Following the bachelor party, the best man has the job of persuading the groom that it is a wiser choice to wed his fiancée than to run off to Rio with Boom Boom, Queen of the Bodacious Ta-tas. He must also be able to reassure the gutless groom that spending the rest of his life with one and only one woman is a good thing. (Okay, he must possess the ability to lie.) Beyond all of that, the best man must con, coerce, convince, campaign, cajole, and coax—to get the groom to the ceremony.

Traditionally, during the ceremony the best man is supposed to hold the ring, the marriage license, and the clergy's fee. Today, however, if you can get the best man to commit to and accomplish one of these three responsibilities (usually holding the ring) it is considered a job well done.

At the reception, the best man is expected to hit on the bridesmaids and the maid of honor, after giving a heartwarming toast that combines the profound realities of marriage in a troubled moral and economic climate with the wit and wisdom of Beavis and Butt-Head or the Three Stooges.

And if he ever remembers, the best man is supposed to return those damn rented tuxedos that have been sitting around his apartment for an extra six weeks to the tune of $800.

The Ushers

♀

The ushers are those friends of the groom that the bride-to-be will, for the next twenty years, be too embarrassed to invite over in the company of her friends or family. Their functions are as follows:

- To make the obligatory jokes about being movie ushers
- To clown around, drink, joke, and flirt with the bridesmaids during all rehearsals and at the wedding
- To wear a rented tuxedo that doesn't fit properly in either the shoulders or the crotch
- To make mock attempts at seating people with the phrase "You can sit wherever you like"
- To escort bridesmaids down the aisle with the traditional "deer caught in the headlights" look on their faces that says "thank God I'm not the one getting married"

Flower Girls and Ring Bearers

♀   ♂

These are roles usually filled by children anywhere from three to ten years of age. Initially, their main duty is to do a wonderful job at all rehearsals, inspiring a sense of confidence in their ability to walk down the aisle. Their main duty at the actual ceremony, however, is to squelch all confidence you had gained in them by whining, crying, and refusing to walk down the aisle in front of actual guests. The promise of anything from Barbie to Nintendo is usually part of the last-ditch efforts to get them to participate.

♥

A Bride's Guide to Wearing White

Although times have changed, and an innocent, pure virgin bride is uncommon, white is still usually the color of choice for the wedding gown. But, if you're not certain whether you feel comfortable wearing white, below is a guide you can follow.

. △

If you have had sex only with the groom-to-be, you should wear white.

But if you and the groom-to-be have an erotic video on the market, you should wear a disguise.

△

If you've been married before, you can still wear white.

But if you've been married more than once, you might wear off-white…which is probably now the color of your white gown saved from the last time.

△

If you've had your share of boyfriends and lovers but are faithful and in love with your groom-to-be, you should wear white.

But if you are in love with your groom-to-be but having an affair with his brother, you should wear something two-tone.

△

If you went through a period of promiscuity in your past, you should wear white.

But if you are still going through a period of promiscuity, you might consider bright red or hot pink.

♥

Buying the Ultimate Dress

At last, your chance to select the gown of your dreams. But where do you begin? Since bridal gowns are rarely part of Macy's holiday sales extravaganza, you're going to have to find a bridal dress shop where

You might find an inexpensive gown at your dry-cleaners.

the staff know exactly what they're doing and understand exactly what you want. But first, you have to figure out what it is you want. The ideal place to begin is with one or two of those twenty-five-pound bridal magazines. There are thousands of dresses pictured and you can simply rip out the ones you like. Then you can rip up the ones that are well beyond your price range or can only be bought from a specialty shop in France. Put aside the ones that "just aren't right for your build" and eliminate those that don't fit your style of wedding (too formal for your informal plans or too casual for your formal wedding). Finally, knock off those to which your friends have responded with "You really like that one?"

Now that you're down to about three gowns you really like, the question is, can the dressmaker give you the circular skirt from one photo, the scalloped neckline from another, and the sequined boarder from the third?

Go to several bridal shops, look at their samples, measure their mannequins, check out their lace, fondle their beads, roll in their ruffles, and frolic in their fabric. As a potential buyer of a $900 dress, you can do whatever you like. Your every whim should be catered to when shopping for a bridal gown.

No carpeted pedestal to stand on? A saleslady should lie down and be your pedestal.

Don't like the lighting? Have them call in an electrician!

Fitting rooms not to your liking? Have them remodeled...add a Jacuzzi! You're the customer spending the big bucks!

This is not just a buying experience—you are forming a relationship with a bridal shop at which you will spend many hours and many, many, many dollars. Here's what to look for in a bridal shop:

1. Avoid any salespeople who snack on garlic.

2. Don't let anyone who's dyslexic take down your measurements.

3. If the only samples in the store are from the Malibu Barbie collection, shop elsewhere.

4. Never trust a dressmaker who uses Krazy Glue.

5. Don't trust a bridal gown shop that offers a two-for-one sale.

6. Never trust a bridal shop that has a car up on a lift.

7. Don't be fooled by a bridal shop that tries to sell you a combination wedding gown/raincoat by London Fog.

8. Avoid any tailor who insists upon escorting you, in his creation, down the aisle.

9. Never shop at a store called Irv's Irregular Bridal Wear.

10. Never trust anyone who says, "I don't have to write it down, I'll remember your measurements."

Some Gown Style Choices

Material: Silk? Satin? Spandex? Corduroy? Polyester?

Neck: V-neck? Off one shoulder? Off both shoulders? Queen Anne neckline? Louis XIV neckline? Low neck? High neck? Turtleneck? Let's get in the backseat and neck? Low cut? Cleavage a-poppin'?

Waist:	Basque waist? Curved waist? Empire waist? Belted waist? Nuclear waste? Bare midriff?
Skirt:	Gathered skirt? Full skirt? Hoop skirt? Mini skirt? Breakaway skirt? Pleated (Catholic-school) skirt? Split skirt? Kilt?
Train:	Chapel train? Cathedral train? St. Patrick's Cathedral train? Choo-choo train?
Trimmings:	Hand-beaded lace? Sheer lace? Chantilly lace? Back bow? Side bow? Butt bow? Bow and arrow? Feather boa? Pearls? Sequins? Sprinkles? Gummy bears?
Color:	White? White? White? White? Off-white? White?
Sleeves:	Short sleeves? Half sleeves? Long sleeves? No sleeves? Extra sleeves? Detachable sleeves? Straightjacket tie-in-the-back sleeves? Uneven sleeves?

All of this is up to you, so go for any and every combination and remember, you pay extra for the alterations and each and every fitting.

Fittings

Your first fitting will be primarily to get your measurements. So from that day forward do not gain or lose a pound; do not bloat, sag, slouch, or alter your shape, weight, walk, or anything about yourself in any way. Don't even see a shrink. Take no chances…the dress must fit!

However, if there have been any added pounds due to wedding-pressure binges, you always have that second fitting to make the appropriate alterations. The dress at this stage will probably not quite fit as you'd like. You can go to a health facility where they will tuck, trim, hem, fold, flatten, and do anything else necessary to *you*—not to the dress—to make it fit. *Or* you can make the seamstress at the bridal dress salon earn those dollars by doing her magic and making it just perfect.

A few suggestions for fittings.

1. Never pat a seamstress with a mouthful of pins on the back.

2. Don't wear Reeboks unless you're planning to walk down the aisle in them.

3. Don't try and see if you can dance in the dress while being pinned.

4. If you change your mind about the beads don't rip them off with your teeth. That's what the seamstress has teeth for.

5. Bring only those whose opinions you really want and who can be helpful to you. Seventeen people including the best man, ushers, and the video guy is usually unnecessary.

By the third or fourth fitting the dress should be just about perfect. You should try to have the dress and the fifth, sixth, and seventh fittings finished at least two or three weeks before the wedding.

By the eight or ninth fitting, you may consider inviting the salespeople and the seamstress to attend the affair—after all, they've had their hands on you more frequently than the groom-to-be.

By nineteen visits you should be ready to take your dress home.

You know you're going for too many fittings when:

1. You start receiving your mail at the bridal shop.

2. The shop owners have asked you to co-sign the lease.

3. You've been given your own private fitting room.

4. They ask your opinions before remodeling the shop.

Getting the Dress Home and Keeping It Safe

Chauffeur-driven limo is the proper way to bring a wedding dress home from the shop; don't let anyone tell you otherwise. Once at home, the dress should be kept at room temperature in a dimly lit but not damp room away from any other clothing and not near a wall. Often it's a good idea to hang the dress on a door that won't be used often. All pets should be boarded at a kennel or with a neighbor until after the big event. The dress should be checked on every twenty-five minutes and the hanger should be rotated twice daily. The train should be lifted and held by at least three people (four is preferable) twice a day but only after everyone has been properly disinfected—use gloves if possible.

No one is allowed to have food within a nine-foot radius of the dress, and children under the age of twelve cannot be in the same room as the dress unless accompanied by at least two adults who have been "dress approved" and briefed on what to do in case of a dress emergency. A security guard is not essential but worth considering if you won't be able to spend a lot of time with the dress.

It's a good idea to find out about ironing the dress, but do not try to do this yourself. Either have the dress shop iron it or take it to a cleaner's, by limo of course, that will iron it for you. *Never* let it out of your sight, even if it means sleeping over in the cleaning store. (NOTE: When you're sleeping at a cleaning shop, the table or counter next to the pressing machines is the warmest at night.

When putting the dress on for the big event, have people wearing white gloves help you. Use the bathroom for the final time, as once you have the dress on, you no longer can use the toilet. Put your makeup on after putting the dress on, with sterilized cloths, towels, and bibs to protect it. If you're worried about the weather, you might wear the protective wrapping the dress came in to get you to the limousine.

Throughout the day, people will kiss you, shake your hand, dance with you, and give you presents. Enjoy the attention, enjoy dancing, enjoy posing for photos, enjoy your wedding, but *never* let them touch the dress!

After the wedding, hang the dress in a closet, well wrapped in a solid, not see-through cover. At your first, fifth, and tenth anniversaries you may choose to try the dress on. Then go immediately to a seamstress and have her sew up all the torn stitches from your "few" added pounds. Save the dress until some family member or friend considers it an heirloom, then let her borrow it, but warn her that you'll inflict the wrath of guilt on her should anything happen to it.

♥

A Few Words About Headpieces

It's important that the headpiece accentuate the bride's head, or at least fit on top of it and remain there while she walks down the aisle. The headpiece can be a wreath, a crown, a decorated Sony Walkman, or an upside-down salad bowl (white, of course).

Headpieces can be pinned to the hair, stapled to the head, soldered to the hair, or balanced on top of the hairstyle if the bride spent years practicing walking with books on her head.

The bride should consider what her hair will look like on the wedding day. A major change of hairstyle can cause a lovely headpiece to become an interesting face mask if it slides out of position at just the wrong time.

Veils are still popular to shield the bride's terrified look as she proceeds down the aisle. The veil is usually lace, but can be nylon or even a solid such as papier mâché if the bride is either very shy or in trouble with the law.

Veils and headpieces are almost entirely white, indicating purity. A red veil or headpiece indicates the bride has been "around the block," a black headpiece indicates that the bride has likened the event to a funeral, and a multi-colored headpiece is a clear sign that the bride has a longing to join the Partridge Family. A purple and black headpiece indicates that the bride has a passion for the Pittsburgh Steelers.

Wedding Trivia:

Why are veils worn?

The veil is traditionally worn to dissuade unwanted relatives from kissing the bride and smudging her makeup prior to the ceremony.

♥

A Very Few Words About Accessories

To accessorize is to spruce up one's ensemble. In this case, it's adding those special final touches to an already striking wedding gown.

Your accessories should be subtle so as not to take away from the dress itself: a single diamond necklace as opposed to a pendant of Snow White and all seven dwarfs, a short single strand of pearls rather than a three-foot chain of pebbles, diamond stud earrings as opposed to nine inches of gold hanging from your earlobes and blocking half the dress.

No matter how much a piece of jewelry costs, other than the engagement ring, the gown is supposed to be the only thing they notice…not even the groom.

A silk bag accompanies many gowns. This is used to put your checks in, or at least a few of them. Hopefully, you'll have room left over, but it's not usually fashionable to carry a silk knapsack.

Accessories to avoid:

Designer scarves
A vest

A giant Snoopy pin
A headband—even if it's white
A black-studded choker, unless you're marrying the leader of a
    motorcycle gang
A feather boa
A backpack
A riding crop
White sunglasses
Wrist sweatbands
A tool belt

And then there are the gloves. The gloves must be white, lace, and very difficult to wash. Leather gloves are generally not fashionable for a wedding, and white mittens are only in vogue in certain parts of northern Canada and in Buffalo, New York.

It's important to make sure all of your accessories complement each other. They must go together perfectly at all times. Thus, if a bead falls off one glove, a bride must think fast and rip a bead from the other glove. If a glove gets smudged or torn, smudge or rip the other one, and so on.

The shoes must also be white. However, since no one will see the shoes under the gown, wear whatever you like. Roller blades give you a nice appearance of gliding down the aisle. The roller blades, however, should be white. Brides have been known to get married in sneakers, sandals, and even clogs. If you do, however, feel that it's important to match the shoes to the gloves to the jewelry to the headpiece, remember that they must remain matched at all times. Therefore, if the gloves lose their beads, so must the shoes.

To sum it all up, less is more, more or less, and more could make them look at the dress less. So if you want to add more, add less than the more you'd add if you needed to add more because you were wearing less. And if that makes any sense, you have the art of accessorizing down to a science.

♥

Ladies' Shopping Day

Like a commander leading the troops into battle, the bride-to-be leads her entourage of soon-to-be bridesmaids (all of whom would be happy

Finding the right bridesmaids gowns takes time and patience.

spending their day at the beach or elsewhere) into the local bridal shop of choice.

Armed with pages torn from bridal magazines, the bride heads her troops through racks of styles and colors designed to accentuate the negative while eliminating the positive. As you weave your way through lace, taffeta, silk, and assorted fabrics that only bridal shops can create, you will hopefully find that one style…that one color…that one dress that you want your bridesmaids to wear at your wedding.

Naturally, once you've found the dress of choice, six of seven bridesmaids will vote you down with a chorus of "You want us to wear *that?*"

And onward you go, leading them along.

When you've finally found a dress that at least a majority approves of (this is one of the few times you'll wish you lived in a dictatorship) and that is within everyone's budget, the fun begins.

This is where the salespeople earn their money with key phrases like "It's you, it's gorgeous" and "We can do something about that, don't worry."

But worry you will as you watch your 5'1", 99-pound niece and your 5'11" 230-pound friend emerge wearing the same dress. How will it look? Can they actually mold, mend, and somehow magically fit one style and color of dress to seven hair styles and colors, contrasting heights, varying bust sizes, etc.? And how many more fittings will there be? Worst of all, how will these seven women pay you back when they get married and put you in a gown of their choice?

♥

Tuxedo Rental Day

Tuxedo rental is often a matter of availability. If they have enough available in the color you want, you and your gang rent it…it's that simple.

Grooms will often initially go with the bride to the tuxedo shop and look at twelve to fifteen models and styles of penguin attire before deciding which one they claim to want. However, not really knowing one tux from another, this is a way of placating the bride and ensuring that she won't return for the fittings—thus getting the groom and his gang out of the process and into watching the ballgame at an accelerated pace.

Since the tuxedos all look alike, and the ushers don't really have any concern other than that they're not priced too high, it's just basically a matter of a few simple measurements. And let's not forget cummerbunds. The purpose of a cummerbund is to show people that you're not getting paunchy. It's either that or a secret desire to have a black belt in karate. After a few quick cummerbund lessons, one not only learns how to work the darn thing, but also how to use it in various other unusual, comical, or obscene manners.

A few words about bow ties. If the tie is supposed to be a phallic symbol, then how does one explain the bow tie? Ouch! Nonetheless, a bow tie is the appropriate consort of the tuxedo. Having selected the matching color, the salesperson may show you several "styles" of bow tie. Since no one other than the salesperson knows the difference, you should take the first style or, to be polite, select the second or third. If upon returning home you find that your fiancée loves the tux, but not the bow tie, assure her that this is the one the salesman said goes perfectly with that very tuxedo; in fact they were designed to go together. She should bow to his bow tie wisdom, since she doesn't know anything about them either.

When going for fittings it's a good idea to wear shoes and not sneakers, a dress shirt and not a turtleneck sweater, and perhaps even a protective cup in case anyone tries to pin anything up.

Beyond that, there isn't much to it. A tuxedo is basically a tuxedo…pick a color and go with what they offer or what the bride likes. After all, think about it: How many guys do you think come walking into a tuxedo shop with pages they've torn out of the bridal magazines themselves?

If you're renting tuxedos, have someone remember to return them. If you're buying tuxedos, buy them in a shop that sells other things (preferably home appliances). That way you can have someone exchange them later for something you might actually use or wear again.

If you already own your own tuxedo, the first thing to do is unroll it from the ball it's been crumpled into since your cousin's ostentatious bar mitzvah three years ago. You then have two choices, either iron it or run it over with your car. Either way, it'll never be completely wrinkle-free. Nonetheless, if you can make it presentable, it's a good idea to try it on just in case those 200 bags of potato chips and 500 beers over the last couple of years have added anything to your gut.

If the tux fits and you can still manage to breathe, you're halfway there. The next step is to either relocate your long-lost cummerbund, or find something in your closet or drawers that you can pass off as a cummerbund. You might be able to substitute a handkerchief folded just so. If by chance you have a white tuxedo, you could probably find someone with a child and borrow a cloth diaper. With a little ingenuity you could make it resemble a cummerbund. However, don't try using Pampers.

Once you've either found, created, or borrowed your cummerbund, you'll need to buy a matching bow tie. Once again, it's only a matter of color, since all bow ties are the same.

The next test is to run all of this past the bride and see if she catches on.

So, there you are at the tuxedo rental shop anyway. Well, at least you've got your own bow tie!

♥

The Wedding Gift Registry: Making It Work for You

Registering at a department store or specialty shop is the perfect way of assuring that your guests will give you exactly what you want at your wedding. It's the polite way of reminding your friends and family that you have good taste and they don't (or at least you're not going to take a gamble). It further assures you of less trips to the returns department of stores in neighboring states where guests saved money on sales tax while choosing color schemes you wouldn't be caught dead with in your home.

It's unfortunate that you are limited to certain stores and selected items (although in many department stores it's a wide selection). It would be nice to open up registries at furniture stores, theaters, luxury hotels, local car dealerships, and banks. There you could put down how much money you expect each guest or couple to give you and they would therefore have to either give the amount or forever be thought of as being cheap.

Generally it is proper to register for the precise amount of settings for a dinner that you would have in your home. For example, if you thought twelve people were the most you might entertain at any given time, you would register for a twelve-piece china set, plus two or three serving dishes, a couple of candlesticks, a couple of bowls and vases, etc.

Nonsense! To paraphrase a cliché, "If you register for it, it will come!" Thus and therefore, you should go for broke, and since *you're* not the one going broke, fill in the number column on the registry with large amounts. Sixteen Orrefors vases, forty-two matching pairs of candlesticks, and twelve decanters are a must for the couple who plans to resell in a big way. Your garage sales will bring in more cash than Macy's Presidents' day sales!

One pattern, one color scheme...again, nonsense! Who wants to use the same color napkins every time guests come over—BORING! Give your guests a choice of crystal, china, and colors. In fact, you should register in as many stores as you can get to in your wedding planning frenzy. And don't forget to check off household appliances. The more you get, the more likely you can start your own Home Shopping Network.

Brides, traditionally, enjoy registering more than most grooms, who are likely to be less concerned with whether the creamer and the sugar bowl match than with who's playing in next year's Sugar Bowl. But it can be fun for the groom if you register his needs too. Don't forget, if you register for it, someone will buy it! So, why not a large-screen television, a VCR or two...or five? And find out if you can register for season tickets. It can't hurt to ask!

It's important to register in advance. This allows you to plan as many pre-wedding get-togethers as possible. A well-planned engagement party is a must, followed by the bridal shower and the wedding-rehearsal dinner party. Even if you usually don't make a big deal about your birthdays, this might be the year to toss in a birthday party for each of you, should they fall during your engagement period.

The longer the engagement the better! This allows for out-of-town relatives to forget that they've already sent you a gift. You therefore send them a second engagement announcement six months after the first. Some relatives will call you, questioning your sanity, to which you'll reply, "I'm so embarrassed. We've been so busy with all the wedding plans."

As for price range…vary your prices, but in the following manner. For example: You want fifty-eight pairs of candlesticks. You choose a $325 pair, a $225 pair, a $125 pair and a $30 pair. No one will get you the cheap pair out of embarrassment. So the worst you'll do is $125. Give them choices, but make the inexpensive choice much too chintzy for anyone with a conscience. Make the next highest choice just a little more than you think the average couple who aren't close friends would spend. Nowadays, that's about $100. Thus you come out $25 ahead on all items from those friends of the family, business associates, and acquaintances. It's also highly recommended, if you want to "milk the registry dry" as suggested, to invite as many people as you know, especially those you're sure cannot attend. But be certain to register in stores that have branches in their cities.

Practice for your upcoming phone conversations:

"I'm so sorry you can't make it, we'll really miss seeing you."

"Send us? Oh, you really don't have to."

"No no, it's not necessary."

"Well if you insist, we're registered at _____."

"I believe there's one on Twenty-third and Main Street right near you in Boise. I understand it's right next to a Dairy Queen, off Route 6; you can't miss it."

Once you've registered, be sure someone is there at all times to sign for and receive packages. If you've over-registered in a huge way, as recommended above, you might choose to start cleaning out the garage ahead of time. Remember, if you register for it, it will come.

♥

The Guest List

Forget about waiting for the proposal—you should start unofficially compiling your guest list as soon as you meet each other's parents. A guest list is generally comprised of several components: bride's family and friends, groom's family and friends, mutual friends, business associates, and those few miscellaneous people you have to invite but aren't exactly sure why—such as children of your parents' friends who invited you to their wedding but whom you haven't seen since. The list may then be subdivided for the sake of limiting the number of guests and for the always challenging task of arranging the seating plan.

Below is a guide you may follow in listing guests by priority.

The Modern Preferential Guest List (In Order of Importance)

✉

Parents
Siblings
Grandparents
Divorced parents' current spouses
Half brothers/half sisters from parents' other marriages
Divorced parents' current lovers (limit three per spouse)
Parents' previous spouses (in descending order)
Personal therapists
Therapy group members
Aunts and uncles who are wealthy
Aunts and uncles you see frequently
Cousins you've met
Relatives you haven't met, but stand to inherit from
Your own ex-spouses
Ex-spouses' current spouses or lovers
Half brother or half sister's spouses, lovers, or inflatable dolls
Wealthy acquaintances
Father's mistress
Business associates
Siblings' cult leaders
Therapy group members' significant others
Parents of the wedding party attendees
Spouses or lovers of divorced parents of the wedding party
Imaginary friends
Domestic help
Pets

While you may have no reservations about inviting your dad's new girlfriend, your mother might not want her in attendance. The same holds true when you invite your father's "traveling secretary" or your mother's sister to whom she hasn't spoken in forty-three years. Therefore, it's important that you check the guest list with parents and siblings. Beyond that it's a free-for-all. It's not your fault if, by coincidence, your prospective sister-in-law had a fling with one of your ushers at a swingers' club in 1982. It's not uncommon that some guests will rediscover someone they've met before. After all, it's a small world.

As for your own personal friends and acquaintances, rule of thumb says that if you were invited to their wedding you should invite them to yours. However, if you haven't spoken to each other in at least five years, or their wedding ended in divorce because of a major fight stemming from your wedding gift, you may also choose not to invite them.

One of the biggest concerns is what to do about guests bringing guests. Who gets invited as a single person and which singles are allowed to bring someone is of major concern. The following is a list you can use to determine who may or may not bring a guest.

1. Wedding party members can bring guests that they've mentioned at least once to their psychologist.
2. Close family may bring guests…especially cousins, so that you can meet the losers they're dating.
3. Distant family and casual friends can bring guests whom they've: slept with at least twice, or introduced to at least one of their parents.
4. Business associates can bring guests influential to your career development. Your boss can bring a guest simply for the sake of future office gossip.
5. Relatives you don't care for can't bring guests. This may either discourage them from coming or entice them into leaving early if they show up.

Although you can't specify the type of guest invited on your invitation, you can, through idle gossip, word of mouth, and mutual contacts, let it be known that you'd prefer your invited guests to bring only those people they feel will mix properly and politely. Try in some manner to discourage anyone from extending the invitation to: .

Someone they met at the bus depot enroute to your wedding

A known international terrorist

A television evangelist or game show host

Anyone who's been banned from a major fast-food chain because his eating habits were scaring away the children

People who think pyromania is an indoor spectator sport

Anyone who's appeared on "Geraldo"

Roger Clinton

Not everyone must be invited to both the ceremony and the reception. You may choose to invite confirmed atheists and casual acquaintances to the reception only. You may choose to invite people with grotesque table manners just to the ceremony.

Children

As for inviting children, there are several options.

You can limit the number of children to those that are yours or your spouse's from previous marriages or from that one wild night in Bermuda...or you can invite only those that your spouse knows about. You should invite the children of your siblings and those from your parents' other marriages. As for the fifteen-year-old babysitter your uncle has developed "a special fondness for," you might choose to decline extending the invitation. It's best not to invite too many children unless you feel it will significantly enhance the amount of money their parents will give you as a wedding gift or unless you're having the reception in a very large outdoor facility with a nearby playground.

Out-of-Town Guests

You might also remember that it's preferable, from the standpoint of receiving more gifts, to research and then invite out-of-town guests who you are fairly positive will be unable to attend. By researching, we mean that you should know that your uncle Arnold has just recovered from a hip operation, is now recuperating in Lithuania, and can't possibly attend your wedding. The act of just sending the invitation will result in the family thinking of you as a genuinely thoughtful individual, while possibly ensuring that he sends you a check or a hundred shares of stock.

Arranging the Guest List

The guest list can be arranged in order of importance, by who you think will and won't be showing up, alphabetically, geographically, or by who you think will spring for the nicest gifts. Some wedding wizards suggest that you keep the names of all the guests on individual index cards, thereby allowing you to utilize such cards for arranging and rearranging and re-rearranging the seating plan. Modern computers are helpful in that they can arrange and rearrange the list in a number of configurations, such as people who've been divorced, people who dress poorly, people you think used to sleep around, etc. Also, if someone is omitted, you can simply respond with, "It was a computer error."

An idea on how to begin the guest list is to first determine the size of the event and then use the previously noted preferential guest list as a guide until you've reached that total number. Once you've reached your original total number, throw the list away, because you've forgotten to invite at least fifteen relatives whom you wish you could forget altogether. Add on the "oh yeah, I guess we have to invite so-and-so" contingency and come up with a new total. Then throw that list away and add on some more forgotten people. Equal input from both sides is a nice idea, but throw it out the window when you realize that you have ten close relatives and your spouse has seventy-one first cousins. Not that you'll invite them, but you'll certainly have to discuss them. Finally, leave a small portion of the list for your parents to invite those infamous "must invite" relatives and business associates that you have either never heard of or simply don't like.

Borderline Guests

These are relatives and friends of the family that you just don't know whether to bother with. In these cases it's always best to yield to another source—a parent or a senior family member. It's important to make sure, however, that inviting a borderline guest doesn't lead to "inviting by chain reaction." This syndrome begins with one added borderline guest and continues to accelerate at an almost unmanageable pace with the phrase "If we invite her then we have to invite him…and if we invite him then we have to invite…" and so on and so on. This can result in a wedding that rivals a national political convention in size and personal warmth.

Last-Second Guests

These are those guests that you wait to invite until after you get a preliminary feel for how many people short you are of the "guaranteed" number you've given the catering hall. These guests include your favorite valet parking attendant, the guy in the mail room whom the bride once had a crush on, the band leader's girlfriend/boyfriend or both, your dentist, internist, or gynecologist, your cat's veterinarian, or the marriage counselor who helped end your spouse's previous state of wedlock.

Definitely Nots

These are the people you've always said you'd never have at your wedding. You don't like them, you wish you hadn't met them or weren't related to them, and there is no way in hell they're going to be at this important day in your life! Well, at least seat them near the kitchen.

♥

Invitations

The invitation can reflect the type of wedding that's being so diligently planned. The invitation will, besides giving the important information, be the guests' first impression of what's to come, so choose wisely.

First, you'll want to choose the color of the paper and the wording. Below are what some of these colors are telling your guests:

⊠

IVORY PAPER WITH BLACK OR DARK BLUE INK: Traditional couple. Nothing out of the ordinary at this wedding, You can set your watch by it—lunch served at one, cake cut at four.

⊠

BEIGE PAPER WITH DARK INK: Not totally traditional, but not exciting in any manner. Bring reading material along.

⊠

LIGHT PINK OR LIGHT BLUE PAPER WITH DARK INK: Expect lots of cute, charming, adorable touches. Bring a barf bag.

✉

GOLD PAPER WITH DARK INK: Keep the word *ostentatious* in mind and prepare for a blatant show of wealth.

✉

RED OR ORANGE PAPER WITH YELLOW OR BLACK INK: This couple is far from traditional. Expect the unexpected, and don't volunteer when the bandleader or DJ asks for someone from the crowd to come on up.

✉

WHITE PAPER WITH WHITE INK: This couple is either stupid or not really sure they want to get married. Call first.

The Cover

And then, of course, there is the cover design. Flowers are a nice touch, his and her hands held together is pleasant, but a skull and crossbones is only considered proper if you're the leader of a well-known motorcycle gang or members of a satanic cult. Trees are a nice environmental message—of course it's more effective if the paper isn't laminated. Scenes like waterfalls, lakes, and shorelines are pleasant if you're planning to take your vows on a boat or in a large bathtub. Pictures of the lovely couple are tacky, and reproductions of famous paintings present the impression that you have more class than you really do or that you're inviting the guests to a gallery opening and not a wedding.

Etiquette and Wording

Wedding invitations have rules and a language all their own.

Proper Etiquette

1. Words that end in "er" or "or" should end in "our," such as *honour, favour, colour, propour,* etc. For example:

Mr. & Mrs. Waltour Wageour
and
Mr. & Mrs. Theodour Millour
request the honour of your
presence at the marriage of
their daughtour
Elenour Tylour
to
Trevour Groegoury

2. Spell out all times and dates—avoid using numbers at all cost. For example:

The wedding will be held on
the nineteenth of April,
Nineteen hundred and ninety seven
at two-thirty at the
Third Avenue Chapel
at Sixteen Hundred and Fifty Seven
Third Avenue, on the cornour of
Ninety-First Street
A reception will follow at the Ninety Nine Club on the
Ninth floor at nine o'clock in the evening

And the envelope should be addressed as follows:

Mrs. Dee Cipher
Four Twenty Seven West Thirty-Third Avenue
Twoson, Arizona, Five two one seven zero
dash eight eight one three

3. It is fashionable to include R.S.V.P. cards inside the invitation. Example:

Please R.S.V.P. no later than March 21st.

_____ I will be attending _____ I might be attending

_____ I will be attending with a guest

_____ I will be attending if I can find a date.

_____ I'll come only if I can't find something better to do.

4. It's polite to include a map to the church or temple and to the reception site. The map should detail the most common routes from various directions. Be specific! An overhead foldout map of the eastern seaboard doesn't really tell people where Glen Cove, Long Island, is or how to get there. On the other hand, you need not detail each and every fast-food restaurant, furniture outlet, and used-car lot they will be passing on a trip from Pittsburgh to Allentown.

5. The invitation should always be in script. If a calligrapher is hired to write out the invitations, guests will call and double check on all of the important details, since a calligrapher's main duties are to write the invitations in a fancy manner and to swirl many letters into illegible variations. The more illegible the invitation, the more formal the wedding will be and the more calls you should receive. If you receive no phone calls, you either wasted your money on a calligrapher or hired one with such expertise that even your phone number was made unintelligible.

   Also, when using a calligrapher, see if she uses Arabic numbers at all. Some only use Roman numerals, which makes your phone number V IV V–III V II VIII.

6. If the couple is hosting (and paying for) the wedding, the proper etiquette to follow when wording the invitation is:

Michelle M. Michaels

and

Michael M. Mitchell

Request the honour of your presence

at their marriage

7. When the bride's parents are divorced but co-hosting:

Ms. Ellen Smith

and

Mr. John Connors and his new wife Whats-her-name
Would like you to favour us with your presence
at the hopefully mour successful marriage
of their daughtour Edna

8. When both sets of parents are divorced, but are hosting:

Mrs. Phillip Fornino, formerly Mrs. Johnson

and

Mr. Everett Johnson and his wife, Clair Stevenson

and

Ms. Collette Madison and her "friend" Wally
(the pool boy)

and

Mr. D. W. Davis the Third and his fiancée,
Candy Blossom
Painfully request your presence at the wedding
of their children, stepchildren or future stepchildren
as the case may be

9. When the bride is pregnant:

Mr. and Mrs. (name withheld due to embarrassment)
request the honour of your presence
at the rather hasty marriage of their
stupid stupid stupid daughter Jessica
to that son of a bitch Rogour

10. When the couple is hosting and they've been living together for a while:

> *Ms. Lynette Palmer and Mr. Josh Baskin*
> *gladly request your presence*
> *as we finally make it legal*
> *to please our parents*

11. Make sure it's clear on the invitation as to when the reception will take place. Examples:

    Reception will follow immediately
    Reception will be held that evening
    Reception will be held two weeks from Friday
    Plans are still being made for a reception: to be announced.

12. All envelopes should be addressed by hand. It's a good idea to find someone or several people with legible handwriting to help you in this endeavor. It's important that the postal carriers be able to discern little things like the difference between Las Vegas and La Vista, Cheyenne and Chicago, and San Antonio and San Diego.

The Typeface

The bolder the typeface, the more you want to get married. Therefore, if people are using magnifying glasses to read your invitation, chances are you're going to eventually be reading some boldfaced divorce papers.

You should also keep in mind that printers love rattling off a variety of fonts and typefaces. They know that you have no idea what they're talking about. Once they open up the big book of fonts, styles, and prices, keep the prices in mind—they're the ones in the **bold type**. Don't feel bad or guilty if you don't like or want the font called "Prestige" but prefer the one entitled "Basic" or even the least expensive font, called "Damn Cheapskates."

You and Your Printer

Since you want to make sure you have enough time, you should contact your printer within minutes after accepting the proposal.

You want to allow time for selecting the invitations, having them printed incorrectly, sending them back, and having them reprinted and sent to you again. After being lost in the post office for a while, they'll finally reach you, after which they'll be addressed and mailed out, then sit around people's kitchens for several weeks. Finally, the R.S.V.P. cards will be returned to you.

It's important to select the right printer for the job.

1. Never choose a printer whose last job was a bar mitzvah, and the family didn't receive the invitations until the boy turned sixteen.

2. Never choose a printer who specializes in printing eye charts or your invitations may look as follows:

MR
ANDMRS
JOHNSIMPSON
REQUESTTHEHONOUR
OFYOURPRESENCEATTHE
WEDDINGOFTHEIRDAUGHTERZELDA

3. A printer who does mostly T-shirts, decals, and bumper stickers also might be wrong for the job unless you want the cover of the invitation to read HONK IF YOU LOVE THIS COUPLE or GETTING HITCHED.

4. Any printer who charges by the letter is questionable.

5. Never trust a printer whose printing press consists of a newspaper and a little egg marked SILLY PUTTY.

Phrases to Avoid on Your Invitations
If you can't make it at least have the courtesy to send a gift
Please attend or we'll never speak to you again
Please try to be nice to the groom

Follow-Ups

Always expect that no matter how clearly marked the R.S.V.P. date is on the invitation, some people will simply not respond. It is therefore up to you to contact these people and find out why they haven't gotten back to you. You have to find a polite way of saying, "Hey, what gives!? How about a response?"

When you do make that phone call you will most likely be met with one of the following responses (keep in mind that what they say isn't quite what they mean):

"I'm sure we sent it out," which means they lost it.

"We weren't sure if we'd be able to make it," which means they're looking for a way out.

"It's so funny that you should call, we were just about to send it out," which means they totally forgot.

"I'm so glad you called, we've been looking all over for the invitation," which means they not only forgot, but had no intention of attending in the first place. (And don't expect a gift.)

"Oh, I'm so sorry, I'm usually so good about those things" means they'll be there, and you can expect a very generous gift since they now feel guilty.

"We never got it" means it's either lost or they're covering their asses. Either way they're now guilted into giving you a nicer gift whether they show up or not.

There are usually a few people whom you've sent invitations to knowing that they won't make the trip just for your wedding. These are usually distant relatives in both respects—you don't know them very well and they're far away. It's always a nice gesture to pawn off these follow-up calls on someone else who couldn't care less about these guests.

When you receive your R.S.V.P. cards, you should immediately begin thinking about who should sit with whom, who will travel to and from the affair together, and who you really don't ever want to speak to again.

One final note: In the envelopes it has become fashionable to include small items along with the invitations. Most popular are pieces of lace, confetti, dried flowers, M & M's, paper clips, rice, watermelon seeds, and lug nuts from the tires of a '63 Chevy.

Sending Out Invitations

Mail out your invitations four to eight weeks prior to your wedding. Give extra time for people out of town. Give additional time to people out of town who are known as procrastinators. Give even more time to people in foreign countries. In fact, you might mail overseas guests an invitation as soon as you've accepted the proposal or when you anticipate being asked.

As for proper procedure, it's very simple:

Address the inner envelope with the married couple's surname or with an unmarried couple's individual names, or with "Guest" if you don't know whom the invitee will bring. Place the inner envelope in the outer envelope addressed to the primary residence and place the R.S.V.P. envelope with your name and address printed on it inside the inner envelope, which is placed in the larger envelope. Place the invitation enclosures in the inner envelope but don't fold the invitations unless they and the inner envelope won't fit in the outer envelope, in which case you should reverse the procedure.

Remember, the inner envelope should be facing up when opening the outer envelope. The enclosures in the inner envelope should be face up in that envelope, which is consequently facedown in the outer envelope. However, if you fold the inner envelope, then face the enclosures down, so that when unfolded they appear face up, unless it's a single-flap envelope, in which case you can place them face up on top of the printed side of the invitation or tucked inside the folded invitation facedown, which will once again be face up when placed in the outer envelope, anyway.

The inner envelope should be unsealed in the outer envelope, which is sealed, and the enclosures should be loose in whichever envelope you put them. Before sealing any envelope, check to make sure you've included the invitation, R.S.V.P. card, the obligatory piece of tissue paper, directions, a raffle ticket, and a stick of gum.

Place a 29-cent stamp on the inner envelope and the outer envelope unless the inner envelope causes the outer envelope to weigh more than an ounce. If an invitation is more than an ounce, add 23 cents per ounce. If the envelope is also too large, then add another 10 cents. If it is less than an ounce but still too large, forget the 10 cents and add 12 cents, unless it's going overseas, then add 95 cents for the first ounce and twenty-three cents for each additional ounce. Or call the guests and invite them by phone.

Now that was easy.

♥

The Seating Plan

Arranging who will sit where sounds like a relatively simple task. At first it's a matter of breaking down the guest list into categories and seating people in conjunction with their category. There is, however, a point in which this seemingly easy routine begins to rival trying to fit square pegs into round holes. Your innocent placing of names at tables will be rudely interrupted by the fact that Aunt Bessy and Aunt Sally haven't spoken to each other in thirty-five years and don't intend to resume speaking at your wedding. Then there's the little-known family facts, such as that about Cousin Jeff being homophobic and Cousin Barry being gay, or about Grandma Gerdy who won't sit at the same table as Aunt Trudy for unknown reasons. You'll even learn some interesting secrets: Your best friend is dating your sister's old boyfriend and your cousin Sheila won't sit near the band out of fear she'll be tempted to take the flutist home with her. Add to all that your thirteen-year-old nephew Mikey who refuses to sit at a kiddie table since he's bringing a date who's twenty-one, and you've got a mess on your hands.

Thus, proceed with caution:

Seating Tips

1. Never seat two people who've slept together but aren't currently doing so at the same table. It doesn't matter how open-minded they say they are, after three glasses of bubbling champagne they're likely to start slinging mud across your expensive centerpieces.

2. Seat either quiet people who won't talk to each other anyway or loud people you really don't want to hear from at the table closest to the band.

3. Try to find a reason for seating everyone at a particular table. Themes are great, but once you run out of themes and good reasons, scrounge for things in common. "Don't they both take Amtrak to work? Great, it'll give them something to talk about" or "Didn't they both belong to Gamblers Anonymous?"

4. Never seat talkative relatives who have known you since birth at a table with your co-workers. You're likely to return to work to find photos of you (age three and in the bathtub) on your colleagues' desks.

5. Don't put the teenagers' table too close to the open bar.

6. Don't be ethnically or socially obvious—the Asian table, the Black table, the Jewish table, the Native American table, the Irish table, the Skinhead table, etc.

7. Remember, whomever you seat closest to the kitchen is least likely to stay in touch with you over the years. Plan wisely. (No, you can't put your in-laws there.)

8. Don't seat heavy people who will block the aisle too close to the dance floor.

Traditionally, tables are broken down into categories such as:

1. Bridal party (often at a dais)

2. Immediate families—together if they get along and will fit at one table

3. Bride's married friends

4. Groom's married friends

5. The ever-popular "single so they'll mingle" table

6. Parents' friends

7. Young relatives

8. Older relatives

9. Co-workers

10. Miscellaneous—people you ride the bus with, your cell mate at Rikers, your cleaning woman, the doorman, etc.

There are, however, other ways in which you might break down the wedding seating arrangements. Here are some alternative table suggestions, and remember, it's your wedding, so have some fun!

Alternative Table Themes

1. People you wish you had gotten naked with before settling down
2. Relatives you thought were dead
3. Co-workers who gossip about each other throughout the day
4. Ex-husbands of your flamboyant aunt
5. People you're fairly certain are in group therapy
6. Friends of yours and your spouse's whom you set up on blind dates with each other...that turned out horribly
7. A mix of diehard Democrats and long-time Republicans
8. People who complain a lot (seat them near the door, by an open window, or by the speaker system)
9. A combination of your father's most wealthy entrepreneurial business associates and your own unemployed friends
10. Gay and lesbian friends with your relatives who idolize Rush Limbaugh or campaigned for Patrick Buchanan
11. The Deal-A-Meal and dieters' table (put them near the kitchen or the cake)
12. Most dysfunctional family members (a sort of reunion table)
13. People you think could snap at any moment
14. Relatives who cough up phlegm a lot

Dealing With the Kids' Table

Since one child's so-called "best behavior" might include setting fire to the cake while another child might consider most of the items neatly arranged on their table to be projectile missiles, you should have a contingency plan for dealing with the infamous children's table should it start resembling a rumpus room.

1. Threaten their parents that you will buy the child a set of drums if said parents do not discipline their youngsters.
2. Engage the children in a game of hide-and-seek. Watch as they run and hide...then don't look for them.

3. Have the clergyperson who performed the service spend the rest of the day in a Big Bird costume.

Seating for the Bride and Groom

Should you choose a dais, you'll be sitting with your bridal party and, if you choose, their guests. Some weddings now have a "guests of the bridal party table" whereby boyfriends, girlfriends, and even spouses of the bridal party members sit at a separate table and have the awkward opportunity to flirt with one another beneath the frequent stares of the bridal party.

Sitting at the center of a dais, a couple gets to witness firsthand the goings-on on the dance floor and at the tables. Guests, however, are often a little leery of approaching you at the dais, perhaps feeling as though they are approaching the bench in a courtroom. If you hold an executive position, you might ease the guests' discomfort by having a secretary seated in front of the dais scheduling times at which the guests might approach you.

Should you choose to sit at a regular table, choose wisely and above all "equally." If you have family from one side you must have family from the other. If you sit with close friends, it has to be *all* your close friends. Any friend left out of the bride and groom's table is now considered an acquaintance and will think of you much further down on their list when they have an extra pair of theater or Super Bowl tickets or are inviting guests to their summer retreat.

To be completely fair, many couples sit alone at a "dais for two" or a "love table." This affords the couple the opportunity to gossip about their guests while being easily approachable and not having to answer to anyone's hurt feelings. Also if you really find that you don't like the food you've selected, you can order in pizza and possibly no one will notice. It's also a good way to start that pre-honeymoon groping under the table without accidentally groping the wrong person.

Table Names and Numbers

Most commonly tables are numbered, but theme weddings, as well as others, sometimes include names for the guests' tables. Here are a few actual examples:

XXX

A couple in Virginia chose twelve flavors of ice cream for their tables. It was noted that one couple who'd been experiencing marital problems were less than amused when they found themselves (quite unintentionally on the part of the bride and groom) at the Rocky Road table.

✗✗✗

One young couple named their tables for the original cast of "Beverly Hills, 90210." Unknown to the guests, they selected their most ornery friends to sit at the Shannen Doherty table.

✗✗✗

A couple in New York labeled their tables by New York landmarks. Rumor has it that when dusk fell upon this afternoon affair, those seated at the Central Park table all got up and left.

♥

The Photographer

Despite the advent of video, still photography remains a paramount part of your wedding planning. The photographer must be well versed at setting up and taking posed pictures as well as capturing those impromptu moments. It's important that you choose someone reliable who understands how significant this day is to you. You don't want someone who will be heard muttering aloud at the end of the day, "Now, which pocket did I put that roll of film in?"

Typically a good wedding photographer should show you samples of his previous work. Below are some key elements to look for when selecting a photographer.

1. A legitimate wedding photographer should not insist on taking nude photographs of the bridal party.
2. A good wedding photographer should not be showing you his collection of combat photos from Desert Storm.
3. Avoid anyone trying to sell you on aerial shots.
4. A wedding photographer should know that the f-stop is not a subway station in New York City.

Use only the most elegant photo studio.

5. Never hire a photographer who uses a kerosene lamp to find his way around the darkroom.

6. A photographer who takes only front shots and profiles of each guest holding a number is a prison photographer, not a wedding photographer.

Most professional wedding photographers provide you with a set of proofs from which you choose the shots you want for the wedding album. There should be a selection of anywhere from 250 to 11,750 proofs for you to look at. And then there are the specialty items offered in the package, such as:

1. Ten wallet-sized photos, three 8 × 10s, a wall-sized poster, and a hologram

2. Three hundred wallet-sized photos, two wall posters, and a billboard on the off ramp to I-95

3. An 11 × 14, three plaques, seventy-two 5 × 7's, and the entire wedding party on an automobile windshield sunscreen

4. Six 8 × 10s, nine 5 × 7's, three 2 × 4's and two dozen T-shirts with an arrow saying I MARRIED STUPID

5. Sixty-three slides and a 3-D poster with the groom's face superimposed on Hulk Hogan's body carrying the bride.

Yes, there are packages to choose from—plenty of them. The idea is to have enough photos to line three rooms of your home, two rooms of each parent's home, and enough left over to hand out on the check-out line at the supermarket.

Costs

The packages are carefully designed to allow you to purchase just less than you need. Whatever else you desire will therefore be extra. For example:

You Want	*The Closest Package*
Five 8 x 10's	Four 8 x 10's
A dozen wallet-sized	10 wallet-sized
Two 11 x 14's	One 11 x 14
50 for your album	45 for your album
25 for each of two parent's albums	20 for each of two parent's albums
	$ 929.00

For the extra 8 x 10, two wallet-sized photos, one 11 x 14, and three slightly larger albums it'll be just an additional $899.00, bringing you up to $1,898 for the nineteen added pictures. But for you, because the photographer likes you, the cost will be only $1,849.

And then there are the "special effects." Close-ups, special filters, the bride and groom framed by a heart, a double exposure of the bride and groom both eating cake, etc. These are all commonly used to add a little something extra. However, you don't need:

1. Your heads superimposed onto the bodies of a bullfighter and a large-breasted peasant girl

2. The photo touched up to make the bride's father resemble Ronald Reagan

3. A photo of you and your spouse framed inside a skull and crossbones

4. An airbrush job that takes away your uncle's $400 toupee.

Equipment

A photographer should come equipped with at least two cameras, a tripod, 600 rolls of film, and enough extra lighting equipment to illuminate the Grand Canyon at midnight. Although some photographers bring along an assistant, you should not be responsible for feeding a photographer, his assistant, nor his entire family from the Netherlands.

Backdrops

Nice backdrops for photos include waterfalls, a spiral staircase, gardens, an attractive chapel, and perhaps a landscape. Don't let the photographer talk you into "creative" shots of you in front of a toxic waste dump, holding up Whoppers in front of the local Burger King, in the reception hall's parking lot, or huddled around a giant neon sign advertising his photo studio.

The Wedding Album

A wedding album is a long-treasured memento of the joyous occasion designed to last a lifetime and to be looked at some 10,000 times the first year and seven times over the next five years. It's important that the book be able to withstand the initial wear and tear. Look closely at the sample wedding albums offered by the photography studio. Make sure they're sturdy—use one as a speed bump in the parking lot, have your spouse and yourself stand on one, let a two-year-old play with one for an hour. If the sample wedding albums can withstand these toughest of tests, then they're ready for the brunt of family and friends browsing the pages.

Thank-You Note Photos

A nice touch is to send a photo along with your thank-you notes. Traditionally this is a wedding photo of the happy couple, posed, poised, and BORING! Surprise your guests—send them candid shots of themselves stuffing their faces at the buffet table, or catching a cat-nap during the ceremony, or caught in a vicious tug-of-war over who gets to take home the centerpiece. These are the photos they'll really enjoy.

Hiring a Pro

Why should you spend the big bucks on a wedding photographer when Uncle Phil has volunteered his services as a gift? For starters, Uncle Phil was only going to give you $25 anyway, so his gift of free photography is worth just that, $25—which doesn't buy much nowadays. But if you aren't sure, compare:

A Professional Photographer	*Uncle Phil*
Uses a tripod.	Has a tripod, but can't get the camera to stay on it without slanting forward.
Changes the film in seconds.	Holds up the processional ten minutes just to advance the film.
Has the photos retouched in a professional lab.	Uses a Magic Marker to fill in the balding area on top of your dad's head.
Gets clear "in focus" shots through a trained photographer's eye.	Gets shots focused through eyes that have seen three martinis and a champagne cocktail.

The Best of the Lot

When you are standing up to your waist in proofs, how do you select the best for your wedding album? Chances are that you have at least 200 proofs you really want, and another 865 that are possibilities. However, unless you're ready to remortgage that new house you just bought or give it outright to the photographer, you can't afford more than the agreed-upon fifty photos. So which ones stay and which ones are dismissed?

To make matters easier, often you should sort the proofs into groups, since photographers traditionally take ten of every shot. This way you'll realize that there are really only about fifty photos to choose from anyway, unless you want seven angles of you cutting the cake and five almost identical shots of you dancing with your father (who didn't really move that much during the dance, anyway).

Below are some rules for the bride to remember while making the decision. (The groom only gets to include two photos: one of himself and his ushers doing something juvenile and one of his parents.)

Rules

1. Although he doesn't get much say in the matter, you do have to include photos of the groom's family and friends. If you're lucky you'll find one big group shot of his entire entourage, thus leaving more room for the important photos of you, your dress, your bridesmaids, and your dress again.

2. Never choose a photo in which your bridesmaids look happier than you do.

3. Only include the "guest table shots" where you posed with the guests or are at least seen in the background.

4. Don't include too many of those impromptu candid circle dancing shots in which you're demonstrating a wide array of facial contortions not seen since the Wild Tea Cup Ride at Disneyland.

5. Carefully separate special-effects photos from those that are simply bad or blurry.

6. Make two special piles of "bride closed her eyes" and "groom closed his eyes" photos. If his pile is higher than yours, yell at him for ruining so many of the photos. If your pile is higher, yell at him for ruining so many of the photos.

7. Select just one of the sixteen angles of the wedding cake.

8. Select just one or two of the twenty-three posed photos of you and your maid of honor.

9. Select just one or two of the thirty-four shots of you and the groom looking lovingly into each other's eyes.

10. Select all thirty-seven of just you in the dress.

Choose only those photos
for your album
that best represent
you as a couple.

Seventy-Five Photos You Shouldn't Do Without

1. Bride climbing out of bed.
2. Bride stepping out of shower.
3. Happy bride at wedding breakfast.
4. Nervous bride leaning over toilet returning wedding breakfast.
5. Frantic bride in slip and bra, with hair in curlers, running around the house screaming at everyone.
6. Bride with mother.
7. Bride with father.
8. Bride with mother and mother's new husband.
9. Bride with father and father's new gay lover.
10. Brother with bride in headlock for old times' sake.
11. Sister with bride in one last hair-pulling fight for sentimentality's sake.
12. Bride putting on her makeup.
13. Bride padding push-up bra.
14. Bride getting splashed as limo pulls up near puddle.
15. Eleven bridesmaids crammed into one limo.
16. Eleven bridesmaids throwing bride's horny younger brother out from moving limo.
17. Groom falling out of bed.
18. Groom bidding farewell to five-foot-high stack of *Penthouse* magazines.
19. Groom leaving for ceremony.
20. Groom returning home, having forgotten to take tuxedo.
21. Groom getting dressed in men's room.
22. Line of guests in cars waiting until your eighty-six-year-old aunt finally gets out of the car so they can pull into the lot.
23. Announcement in front of church or temple that couple is getting married. One of the couple's last names misspelled.
24. Bride using karate-kick motion to inform groom in no uncertain terms that she doesn't want him to see her until she walks down the aisle.

25. Bridesmaids lining up for processional.

26. Ushers getting stoned in the men's room.

27. Bride's mother and groom's mother wearing almost the same exact dress and obviously not pleased about it.

28. Processional—bridesmaids look serene, ushers panic-stricken.

29. Best man checking pockets to relocate ring.

30. Groom scrunched between parents as they walk aisle too narrow for three.

31. Groom standing alone with "walking the last mile" expression.

32. Bride about to descend aisle blocked by video guy.

33. Bride and father descending aisle blocked by video guy.

34. Groom meeting bride halfway up aisle blocked by video guy.

35. Bride, groom, and video guy walking final steps of aisle.

36. Bride and groom exchanging vows

37. Bride and groom exchanging wanton glances.

38. Bride and groom trying to shove rings onto each other's trembling fingers.

39. Groom trying to kiss the bride through the veil before remembering to lift it.

40. The kiss blocked by the video guy.

Some posed shots will include:

41. Bride and groom's hands.

42. Bride and groom's feet.

43. Bridal party forming a human pyramid.

44. Bride alone with big grin as groom hides under gown.

45. Ushers making obscene gestures while posing with groom.

46. Full bridal party shot featuring paired couples who walked aisle together trying to look as if they know and like one another.

47. Bride with groom's parents.

48. Groom with bride's parents.

49. Groom's mother with bride's father.

50. Bride's sister with groom's mother.

51. Groom's father with bride's sister's boyfriend.

52. Bride's mother with groom's grandmother and groom's father's second wife.

53. Groom's brother with bride's grandfather and golfing caddie.

54. Groom's sister with bride's father and video guy.

At the reception:

55. Bride, groom, and waiter carrying tray enter together.

56. Groom steps on bride's feet during first dance.

57. Bride dancing with her father.

58. Groom dancing with his mother.

59. Bride dancing with groom's father.

60. Groom's father dancing with seventeen-year-old cocktail waitress.

61. Aunt Shirley spills punch on herself.

62. Bandleader grabbing his crotch during version of Michael Jackson's "Beat It."

63. Bride and groom kissing at table.

64. Bride and groom's hands active under the table.

65. Guests with a vast array of awkward facial expressions as they try to keep pace during hora and other circle dances.

66. Bride's grandmother asking bandleader not to play so loud.

67. Bride throwing bouquet.

68. Seven-bridesmaid pileup on floor to catch bouquet.

69. Groom taking off bride's garter with video guy on knees getting extreme close-up.

70. Bride and groom with gobs of cake dripping from their mouths.

71. Guests stampede as Viennese table is presented.

72. Bride, groom, and video guy wave good-bye at door.

73. Bride and groom changing into traveling clothes.

74. Guests waiting in long valet parking lines.

75. Blurred shot of back of bride and groom's limo as photographer gets bumped by guest in car anxious to get out of the parking lot.

These are just some of the photos you *must* have.

Of course there will also be those photos that your folks must have and those that they have to send to their friends. The ever-popular photos of each and every guest table are always popular giveaways to people who attended the wedding. These photos are always taken twice and only after the photographer has carefully lined everyone up perfectly with one brilliant expression that sums up fourteen years of photographic expertise: "Why don't the four of you go stand behind the four of them?"

Wedding Trivia:

But why do they always take the shot twice?

The first of the guest-table shots is designed to get someone either still chewing or looking away from the table. The second is taken specifically to get the waiter or busboy leaning into the shot.

♥

Waiting for the Photos

It is reasonable to assume that it will be several weeks before you see the wedding proofs. It is reasonable to assume that you have several weeks to choose the proofs you want copies of and the ones you want in your album. It is reasonable to assume that the photographer will be paid during this time period. Therefore it should be a reasonable assumption that you'll soon see your wedding album. WRONG!

The putting together of your wedding album is a slow, patient process that takes place when the photographer "gets around to it." Rocket ships have been built, wars have begun and ended, and marathons have been run in less time than it takes to put together a wedding-photo album. The sad truth is that there have been wedding albums that have taken so long to be assembled that the couple has divorced in the ensuing time. Here are some handy tips that tell you perhaps it's time to start bugging the photographer.

You Know the Wedding Album's Taking Too Long When:

1. You find yourself telling your children, "We'll have it any day now."
2. You can't remember the names of the people in the photos.
3. You're no longer friends with most of the bridal party.
4. You're planning to give it to your spouse as a tenth anniversary present.

But you do want a job well done. A good wedding-photo album:

1. Has your wedding photos in it and not someone else's.
2. Doesn't say SPIRAL LOOSELEAF NOTEBOOK on the front cover.
3. Doesn't start with the "Couple Saying Good-bye" photo.
4. Doesn't include a pop-up centerfold of your uncle Sherman in drag.
5. Doesn't have six or eight photos fall out every time you open it.
6. Shouldn't have a $1.99 sticker on it.
7. Shouldn't be interspersed with autographed photos of the Atlanta Falcons' starting defense.
8. Doesn't come in plain paper wrapping.
9. Shouldn't have a photo of Manuel Noriega on the cover.
10. Should not be held together with staples and Elmer's Glue.

♥

Videotaping the Wedding: Finding the Right "Video Guy"

Videotaping the wedding, and most other occasions, has become part of the American Custom. No video, no documented proof that your great-aunt actually got up and did the hora or tarantella. No video, nothing to torture visiting friends and relatives with for the next six months. No video, no official remembrance of Uncle Fred dancing on a chair with a flower in his teeth. Therefore, you have to have the big event on everlasting videotape…plenty of copies available.

There are various ways one can shoot your wedding video and it's important that you explore and understand the options—after all, you'll be charged for them.

You can opt for the straight one-camera video following the events of the wedding from start to finish. If that's too dull, you might add interviews with guests. Still too dull? You might spring for a two-camera shoot, allowing the video camera editors to work in various scenes from the footage shot by each camera. More, you say? How about a little background on the bride and groom? Let's add those pictures of you as children, with "The Way We Were" or "Memories" playing along with the photos. Still not quite right? How about special effects? Technology can do wonders, why not go for the whole package? In fact, you can even work in some of that honeymoon footage at the end. Spare no expense, go for it all, and your video should be nominated by the Academy for best wedding video, shot at a cost of thousands. Is it really all that simple? Let's explore further.

Censored

Some clergy will not allow cameras to film in the church or temple. This is actually not because of any religious custom; it's usually because friends or relatives took up a collection and promised to donate this vast sum of money to the youth program if the clergy would ask you not to video the service.

It's a frequently used ploy, by those who know that you won't question your rabbi, priest, or minister's intentions, and it spares friends and relatives from the tedious watching of the ceremony over again. It also gives them a chance to see, in person, you getting married as opposed to the back of the video guy.

Interviewing the Guests

Traditionally, this is done exactly at the time the guests are eating their main course. The trick is to catch as many guests with food in their mouth as possible. This allows for marvelous footage of Uncle Norman wishing you years of happiness with a buttered roll between his teeth and Aunt Jenna accidentally projecting a piece of broccoli as she wishes you as marvelous a marriage as she and Uncle Phil have had. Uncle Phil, meanwhile, is too busy eating. It's also a great opportunity to catch people off guard, which results in wonderful bloopers and blunders that you can send to "America's Funniest Wedding Videos" at a later date.

It's a good idea to suggest questions to the video guy. ("The video guy," by the way, is the technical term by which he's known.) If you don't plan ahead you never know what he'll ask the guests. Below are some questions video guys have been known to ask:

1. Did you ever think you'd see them getting married?
2. Have you ever seen either of them naked?
3. Which of them do you think will be the boss in their house?
4. Do you think they ever wear each other's clothes?
5. Can I have your fruit cup while you're talking into the mike?
6. What excuse were you planning to use to get out of coming today?
7. How much are you giving them as a gift? Do you think it's enough?
8. Which of you is making the bigger sacrifice to be here at this lovely wedding today, you or your husband/wife?

The Two-Camera Job

Two cameras are nice, but how much more equipment will they bring? Video guys get excited when you ask for a two-camera shoot and start adding additional lighting people, a guy with a boom microphone, and even someone with a slate to start the proceedings with "Ready, set, start walking the aisle." The problem, however, is that while all of this may look good on video, it's intrusive on and around the dance floor. Circle dancing is supposed to be done around the couple, not around two guys standing on ladders getting overhead shots and appropriate lighting. Unobtrusive is the key word for a video guy. Remember, you don't want to turn to kiss the bride only to smack your lips against a zoom lens.

The Nostalgic Touch

It's a pleasant touch to see a handful of photos of bride and groom in their formative years. A couple of shots on the playground swings, a bar mitzvah or communion photo…perhaps a graduation shot and one or two of the happy couple before they began the exhausting wedding planning process.

Unfortunately, some couples don't adhere to the idea that less is more, and decide to give you a more thorough synopsis of their backgrounds individually and together. The "busy" twenty-five–photo montage of the bride and groom's formative years:

Photo #

1. Bride's mother pregnant.

2. Infant groom in hospital maternity ward.

3. Infant bride being breast-fed.

4. Groom's first successful potty display.

5. Bride in baby carriage. Back of carriage has cans tied to it by her mother.

6. Three-year-old groom at home plate holding bat incorrectly. Father in background cheering him on.

7. Bride playing fairy princess in first-grade pageant. Mom looks thrilled.

8. Groom playing fairy princess in first-grade pageant. Dad looks worried.

9. Bride dressing Barbie in bridal outfit.

10. Groom catapulting G.I. Joe out of backyard tree house.

11. Bride leaving drugstore having purchased first "feminine" product.

12. Groom sits in principal's office after sneaking into girls' bathroom.

13. Bride in first formal strapless gown. Dad trying to cover her with his sport coat.

14. Groom with older cousin Sheila at her Sweet Sixteen party. He holds Mexican sombrero in front of his pants to block involuntary response to well-developed cousin.

15. Bride graduating high school with honors.

16. Groom with pals in summer makeup class.

17. Braless bride runs from cops with college pals in protest march.

18. Bleary-eyed groom returns home after pledging fraternity still wearing nun's habit and stiletto heels. Dad looks worried again.

19. Bride with first post-college boyfriend. Mom in background measuring him for a tuxedo.

20. Groom and first post-college girlfriend. He looks worried; she looks pregnant.

21. Bride and groom together on early date. Bride's mother in background on phone to catering hall.

22. Bride in peek-a-boo bra and panties (oops, how'd that get in there?).

23. Bride and groom at engagement party. He looks worried. She looks pregnant.

24. Bride at bachelorette party licking ice cream off the chest of a Chippendale's dancer. The dancer looks worried.

25. Groom with coat over head outside bachelor party just raided by the vice squad. The exotic dancer looks worried.

All this to the music of Paul Anka.

And then, after just twenty minutes, it's on to the actual wedding footage...

Special Effects

Thanks to Steven Spielberg, among others, we've become indoctrinated with special effects. If we don't see at least one car blow up and a person slowly transformed into a slimy creature from the great beyond, we feel as if we've been cheated.

So what can they do with a wedding video?

Aerial shots are nice at an outdoor event, especially with the circle dances. Some brides, meanwhile, have agreed to wear the new Veil Cam, which is a tiny camera in the bride's veil to capture the entire event from her perspective.

That first dance can now be slowed down to show everyone that those sixteen ballroom dancing lessons were worthwhile after all, and the bride and groom can dissolve into the tiny figures on top of the cake. Another popular favorite is to frame the couple inside of a heart, or perhaps a dollar sign or even a condom, depending on the theme of the relationship. Special-effects reaction shots include the popular "head spinning around" response to the "Do you take so and so to be..." part of the vows. It's quite comical and effective.

Sixteen images of the bride and groom dancing around the screen while the best man is making the toast is just another way of saying, "Gee, look at technology. Isn't it wonderful how much it's raising the cost of our simple video?"

One of the latest techniques is to merge the bride and groom's features and create the loving-couple hermaphrodite. This answers the nagging curiosity of all those guests who'd been wondering what they'd look like if the loving couple were just one person.

So there you have it, a summary of what is available to highlight your wedding video.

Below are a few more tips for you to keep in mind when selecting the right video guy.

1. If the only previous work he has to show you involves two midgets, a nude couple, and a three-gallon drum of Reddi Wip, perhaps this person is new to the wedding-video business.

2. Make it clear what you do and don't want on your tape. "We want the vows, but taping ends when the honeymoon begins."

3. Read your written contract carefully. Know who's liable if that special moment when your drunk uncle fell into the wedding cake suddenly appears on one of those television blooper shows.

What You Don't Want on Your Video

1. Trick photography that makes everyone look like George Burns

2. The tape set to the soundtrack of *The Three Stooges Do Gershwin*

3. Spliced-in footage of the building of the Alaskan Pipeline

4. The video guy's finger.

5. A documentary narrative on the state of matrimony in America today by Regis Philbin and Kathie Lee Gifford

6. "The Battle Hymn of the Republic"

7. Commercials

8. The voice of Don Pardo

9. Your niece or nephew singing the long version of "MacArthur Park"

10. The video guy's toll-free phone number

Ten Ways to Trick Your Friends Into Watching Your Wedding Video

1. Blackmail.

2. Tell them that they're featured in some candid moments.

3. Sneak it in during the Super Bowl halftime show.

4. Tell them there'll be nude scenes.

5. Threaten them with something worse, like *Ishtar* or *Ace Ventura, Pet Detective.*

6. Serve a lot of alcohol prior to turning on the set.

7. Keep saying "Wait, wait, the good part is coming up."

8. Tell them it's an Infomercial.

9. Point out people they missed in the background like Billy Crystal, Arnold Schwarzenegger, and Cher.

10. Don't offer any food until they've watched it.

Seven Ways to (Politely) Get Out Of Watching Someone's Wedding Video

1. Blackmail.

2. Beat them to it—put a tape of your vacation in Boise in the VCR before they get the wedding video in there.

3. "Accidentally" overload their electrical circuit and blow a fuse (make sure it's the right one).

4. Fake food poisoning—keep running to the bathroom.

5. Drink a lot of alcohol and pass out.

6. Use the "We have a babysitter" excuse whether you have children or not.

7. Keep your host busy serving so you can unobtrusively hit fast-forward again and again.

♥

Finding the Wedding Band or DJ

Wedding bands generally consist of struggling musicians who have other jobs during the week. They showcase for you, and you choose according to what you hear and what you see. For example, a group that sounds terrific but resembles the Grateful Dead before their morning showers might not be quite right for a formal gathering. On the other hand, a group that looks quite ideal for a wedding but performs only the greatest hits of Ray Stevens might be a little limiting.

Besides sounding and looking good, the personality of the band-leader is something to take into account. Basically you want someone who can act as a master of ceremonies without overdoing it, someone personable yet not obnoxious, glib but not gross, entertaining but not tacky.

Below are some of the common bandleader personalities to avoid:

♪

The Center-of-Attention Type:

This is the guy who has totally forgotten that it's your wedding and believes that he's up there to steal the show. He's easy to spot. He's a frustrated middle-aged singer, sporting a greaser hairstyle while trying to emulate Tom Jones.

♪

The Center-of-Attention Party MC:

Confused that this is a children's party, this is *the* most obnoxious type of bandleader. He is convinced that he has to be doing something to keep you amused and entertained at all times. Between picking on assorted guests, constantly urging everyone to clap hands and "party," and infusing bad jokes into their set, this guy has every table moving farther and farther from the bandstand. Plus, he can't sing!

♪

The Showstopper:

Often a female lead with a great voice and dreams of becoming another Mariah Carey, this is the lady who bursts into riveting solos, punches powerful high notes, and turns a simple "The Bride Cuts the Cake" into the final scene from *Madam Butterfly*. Remind her early on that there will be no one in the audience who can help her career.

♪

The Lawrence Welkers:

A dying breed, these are the mellow, a-one-and-a-two band-leaders who just smile occasionally to remind you that rigor mortis hasn't set in. These are the rare few who can make "Born to Run" and "Blue Moon" sound alike.

§

The Schmaltzers:

It's enough that the ceremony is beautiful and has brought numerous guests to tears, but you don't need this guy laying it on with gobs of syrupy sentiment that'll have your guests weeping into their fruit cups.

§

The "Too Hip" DJ:

Yes, you want to get everyone boogying on the dance floor, but no, you don't need someone calling your grandparents "Those Bad Ass Old Folks With a Hip Hop In Their Walkers."

Some Tips on Finding the Right Band Or DJ for Your Wedding

1. Never trust a bandleader who's an accountant during the week to get the crowd up and dancing.
2. If the band wears marching uniforms and has a tuba player, they're not a wedding band.
3. If by Sinatra, they think you're requesting something by Nancy, don't hire them.
4. If, when you go to audition them, you can hear them from two miles down the road and you're inside a 7-Eleven, they may be just a little too loud for your wedding.
5. Never hire a band that claims to have a guy who can play the entire score from "West Side Story" on a flügelhorn.
6. A string quartet usually does not mean three guys with banjos and one with a rubberband.
7. Make sure the band you see is the band that's going to show up. Don't let them switch a good drummer for a guy whose only experience is playing the chopsticks on the table while waiting for dinner at a Chinese restaurant.

8. A band that looks and sounds like Metallica may have a hard time with the hora and other traditional dances.

9. Don't hire a DJ who breaks for weather and traffic updates during the reception.

10. The DJ shouldn't rap along with the Wedding March.

♥

The Flowers

Note: Before reading the section on flowers and selecting a florist, you should note that 99 percent of grooms do not participate initially in this part of the planning. After coaxing, threatening, bartering, and compromise settlements, 98 percent still do not participate in this part of the planning.

Flower Selecting

Flowers are selected to beautify the wedding, add a sense of nature, and remind the groom that the bride expects him to buy her flowers at least six times a year.

Below are guidelines to follow when flower shopping:

🌹   🌹   🌹

1. If a flower brings tears to your eyes, chances are it's not sentiment but allergies.

2. A rose that has no smell is either dead or plastic.

3. A good florist doesn't deliver two weeks before the wedding.

4. Never select a bouquet that held at your waist will block out your face.

5. Select the appropriate flower for the groom, the best man, and the ushers. If left to their own volition, the groom will show up wearing a flower-shaped room deodorizer and the ushers' flowers will squirt water or even beer.

6. Choose less appealing, less attractive flowers for the bridesmaids than for yourself.

7. Since this is your big chance to indulge in flowers, decorate as many places as possible with floral arrangements, including arches, canopies, candelabras, centerpieces, the limousine dashboard, the ladies' room, the band's drum set, your mother-in-law, the cake, the steaks, the potatoes, and that unattractive FIRE EMERGENCY EXIT sign.

8. Don't trust a florist who doesn't know the difference between a dozen lilies and poison oak.

9. Include very few thorns in your throw bouquet.

10. Choose flowers that have at least a 50 percent chance of lasting through the day.

11. Avoid flowers that you have to cut out of a book.

12. Never choose a florist whose idea of a centerpiece is a wreath that says "Congratulations to a fine mare."

13. A rose by any other name is a rip-off, so don't fall for it.

14. And finally, remember, don't involve the groom in any of this.

After the wedding you may choose to keep your bouquet in the refrigerator until your first wedding anniversary, when you eat it.

Flowers and Their Symbolism

Flowers not only look beautiful and smell delightful, but they say something about who you are.

Flower	*What It Says About You*
BABY'S BREATH	Pure of heart, somewhat frugal, overanxious to start a family
CARNATION	Faithful, enjoy instant dairy products, commonplace, ordinary, dull, eat at Denny's
DAFFODIL	Carefree, sway with the wind, no mind of your own, get into automobiles with strangers
DAISY	Cheerful, perky to an almost intolerable level, watch Regis and Kathie Lee
IRIS	Faithful, wise, classy, with hidden wealth, high SAT scores
IVY	Faithful, good companion, went to good school, ambitious, good chance you'll cheat on each other
LILY	Virtuous, elegant, with many credit cards, don't like to be touched by people you don't know well
ORANGE BLOSSOM	Have eternal love, want to move to the South, seek out the answers to unexplained questions (like why are orange blossoms white?)
ROSE	Seek love, romance, cry during movies (even comedies), consider Valentine's Day most important day of the year
TULIPS	Ideal lover, seek mutual orgasm, have credit line at erotic bakery

♥

The Cake

No matter how wonderful the wedding, people will remember the cake above all else. It's one of the last elements of the wedding and people should remember how beautiful it looked. Taste is secondary to appearance. In fact, the better it looks, the better people will think it tastes. It's known as the "Cake Illusion." In some cases it's more than an illusion, as a beautiful-looking cake made of Plexiglas is shown, but not eaten—thank goodness.

Therefore, it doesn't matter what the cake they see tastes like. With nine other desserts, trays of cookies, and even a Viennese table, people aren't there to eat the wedding cake, just look at it.

Multi-tiered wedding cakes are popular, with pillars to hold the layers up—it's a sort of Frank Lloyd Wright cake style. On the top stand the miniature bride and groom. The extremely wealthy have cakes so huge that they hire relatively short couples to actually stand on top of their cakes. But, as we progress, we no longer see just a bride and groom standing on top of the modern wedding cake. One couple had the bride, groom, wedding party, and significant others standing on top of a cake that more closely resembled a crowded elevator than a wedding reception.

Specialty Cakes

✿

The Marriage of Convenience Cake is actually two entirely different cakes put together with a plastic bride and groom on different tiers both talking on cellular phones.

✿

The May/September Cake, (he's sixty-three, she's twenty-three) is a rich chocolate cake lined with milk of magnesia but covered with sprinkles. The bride figure is reaching into the wallet of the groom figure, who's reaching for an oxygen mask.

✿

Figurines on top of second marriage cakes often have statues of their ex-spouses standing behind them chuckling.

✿

The "I Married an Alien" Cake is shaped and decorated as a giant green card.

✿

The Marrying for Money Cake is, of course, a sponge cake.

✿

A cake for two marrying politicians is that rare blend of decorative toppings filled entirely with hot air.

✿

The Dr. Ruth Wedding Cake is any kind of "short" cake with the plastic bride and groom doing any number of things in any number of positions.

SPECIAL DESIGNS

Cakes have been made in any number of special shapes and sizes, often representing something special to the couple. Some popular cake designs in recent years have included the Eiffel Tower, the Leaning Tower of Pisa, the Empire State Building, and even the Seattle Space Needle. Today cake makers are doing amazing things with cake designs. Some of the most popular designs in the early 1990s include the "Actual Size" Ross Perot Cake and the Satellite (Deep) Dish Cake, which comes with a remote control cupcake for the groom to hold.

Cake Etiquette

It's important to pose for pictures with the cake. Therefore, you must remember a few basic rules of cake etiquette during the reception. First, it's okay to taste the icing with your finger when no one's looking, but it's not appropriate to suck away an entire tier while the guests are occupied doing the tarantella. It's also not considered proper wedding etiquette to cut the cake, stand back, and yell, "Come and get it!"

Cake Customs

The bride and groom are supposed to cut the cake together while their guests generally sing "The Bride Cuts the Cake" and "The Groom Cuts the Cake" to the tune of "Farmer In The Dell." The couple then feed each other slices of cake. The bigger the slice, the more say you'll have in the marriage. Of course, if that were true you would see couples trying to gulp down the entire top layer, figurines and all.

Once bride and groom are fed, the cake is generally whisked into the kitchen or off into some corner where it is cut to serve to all the guests. Catering halls and restaurants have been known to fool their customers by switching cakes, so you must watch that they serve the cake you ordered.

Five Ways to Tell If They're Serving the Right Cake

It's the old switch-a-roo if:

1. Someone gets a piece with the writing "Mazel Tov on Your Bar Mitzvah Bernie" on top of it.
2. The cake they're serving comes in individually wrapped packages marked "Twinkies."
3. They try to convince you that the butter cream you're eating is actually chocolate mousse.
4. You catch the waiters sneaking thirty-two Sara Lee carrot cakes in through a fire exit.
5. The vanilla icing on the cake now tastes and looks exactly like mint julep.

Buying the Cake

A wedding cake is a major purchase and you should get exactly the type of cake you want. Ideally your cake should be a combination of rich chocolate, fruit for the health conscious, low-fat whipped cream for the weight conscious, rum for those looking to be unconscious, and a frosting that matches your color scheme. The cake should be several tiers high with perhaps a waterfall, heliport, or French chateau on top, depending on whether you want to convey a "romantic" setting or a "couple on the go" image. There should also be plenty of flowers and, of course, the figurines.

A cake need not be round anymore—you may choose any shape you like. However, a word of caution. To most bakers, oblong means round, oval means round, triangular means round, pentagonal means round, and rectangular usually means square...and often square means round. They're used to making round cakes, but if you're lucky, square ones are within their repertoire.

You should shop around and settle only on a baker who treats you properly and patiently, allowing you to sample and taste everything in the shop from custard pies to sourdough bread. No, these have no bearing on your cake, but if you're going to spend several hundred dollars, what's a little free sample or ten?

You can ask around, look at cake photos, and even do some taste testing, but ultimately you have to decide if this is the baker you want making one of the most important cakes in your life...a cake that

"Are you sure this is the right cake?"

symbolizes who you are as a couple and how the world should view you and treat you…a cake that exemplifies your love for one another, your devotion, your innermost feelings, wishes, and desires…a cake that makes people stand up and take notice!

Ten Tips on Finding the Right Baker

1. Anyone who's about to sell you a $2,000 specially made cake should not start out by telling you to take a number and wait to be served.

2. Never trust a baker who makes cheesecake with Velveeta.

3. Be wary of a baker who charges extra for bakery string.

4. Never trust a baker who always smells of varnish.

5. If the photos show thirty-eight different couples posing with the exact same cake, be suspicious.

6. If you order a marble cake and the baker wants to know how many marbles to include, cancel the order.

7. A legitimate baker should not need to take the bride's measurements.

8. Be careful of any wedding cake baker who says, "If you don't like it, next time I give you a free one."

9. A good baker does not offer to throw in sequins.

10. If a baker rattles off a list of ingredients and it includes asphalt, find another baker.

♥

Limousines

Arriving at your wedding via chauffeur-driven stretch limousine is most fashionable. Limousine services generally charge by the hour and provide a luxurious vehicle for you to arrive and depart in. But there's a lot more you should know about hiring and riding in limos, and since most of us don't ride in them often, below is a guide to what you should be aware of.

Consumer Guide to Limousines

1. If the vehicle has the company's phone number printed on the side, it is not an elegant limousine.

2. There should not be other passengers in the car waiting to be dropped off at the racetrack and other locations.

3. Don't be taken in by any company that sends you two black Volvos, parks them close together, and insists it's a stretch limousine.

4. If the car is a black Cadillac station wagon, it's a hearse, so send it back.

5. Never pay to ride in a limousine with a STUDENT DRIVER sign on the top.

6. A limo shouldn't have a meter running.

7. A luxury limousine shouldn't have a giant plastic insect on the roof.

A Little Bit About Chauffeurs

1. The chauffeur's kids should not be in the car, along for the ride.

2. The chauffeur should not ask if you'd like to drive.

3. Often chauffeurs think they know the best routes. Don't let a chauffeur take you from Los Angeles to Malibu by way of Las Vegas.

4. A good chauffeur shouldn't make the bride get out and pump gas.

5. The chauffeur need not be invited to the reception, even if he insists he hasn't had time for breakfast.

6. A good chauffeur won't challenge other drivers to a drag race.

Limousine Etiquette

1. Don't hang out the windows yelling and waving to the entire neighborhood (only at select homes).

2. Never hurl champagne glasses from a moving vehicle.

3. Don't stash cocktail franks under the seat cushions.

4. Don't crush ice cubes by opening and closing the between-seat divider.

5. It's wrong for the bride to have a final last-minute fling with the chauffeur. (Let a bridesmaid do it.)

6. It's proper to tie tin cans to the back of the vehicle, not to your future in-laws.

7. When riding to the affair, should your vehicle get cut off by another driver, try to refrain from giving him the finger or yelling obscenities, as it's likely to be one of your guests or your priest or rabbi.

Coming and Going

Limousines are not the only means of transportation to and from a wedding. The bride and groom may choose to come and go in any number of ways ranging from dog sled in Alaska to Kiack in Hawaii. But what does your mode of transportation tell your guests about you as a couple?

Hot Air Balloon: The environmental couple.

Hang Glider: The somewhat insane environmental couple.

Leaving by Helicopter: Anxious to get to the honeymoon.

Chartered Plane: Anxious to get the honeymoon activities off to a flying start.

Horse and Carriage: Romantic couple who enjoy things at a slow pace…and love tying up traffic for miles.

Arriving on Horseback: Outdoors couple who loved the movie *City Slickers* and don't really care how they smell on the receiving line.

Arriving Via Roller Blades: A couple who have been living in Southern California too long.

Rented Sports Car: He got a say in the wedding plans.

No matter how you get there, it's only important that you get there…and in one piece. One groom thought it would be entertaining to be shot into the festivities by a cannon. And, when it was time for the groom to arrive, he was indeed seen flying through the air, toward a well-padded landing area just north of the altar. It was a dramatic entrance and the wedding probably would have been somewhat of an event too had he not landed slightly south of the altar onto a row of the bride's relatives. The couple left the site via ambulance and were married at the nearby hospital, where he was released with some broken ribs after a few days. The relatives were also fine, but talk about getting off to a "flying start" with your in-laws!

It's important that whoever or whatever is getting you to and from the wedding is arranged for well in advance. Millions of viewers watched the famous wedding episode of the hit television series "Rhoda," in which the title character took the New York City subway into the Bronx, complete in gown, to get to her own wedding.

Another nice idea is to know how to get to the church, temple, catering hall or wherever the site may be. If while driving to a backyard wedding in a cozy residential section of town you suddenly find yourself on a dead-end street surrounded by steel refineries, you may indeed be lost.

One "groom" in Chicago not only got lost, but wound up at the wrong church. Nervous about being late, he ran in and hastily lined up to walk down the aisle. Only after several of the ushers surrounding him looked at him curiously did he realize that they were not his ushers and that this was someone else's wedding. It was a good thing he did, or the bride would have been in for a rude awakening on the honeymoon.

♥

Attendants' Gifts

All members of the bridal party should receive gifts as a show of gratitude on your part. After all, they've spent hundreds of dollars of their own money and hours of their time on your wedding. Therefore, the only appropriate thing to do is to honor them with a tie clasp or fancy letter opener.

Your objective is to buy the same item for each of the men in the bridal party and the same item for each of the women. Therefore, you need to find, in quantity, something that looks attractive and costly which they will never use. To be certain that they cannot later pawn off your gift to them as a meaningless but attractive present to someone else, it is advisable to have it engraved with their initials. Some attendant's gift ideas include:

- Stylish pens that are hard to find refills for

- An appointment book for the year that you're already half way through

- Bottles of wine for your friends who've just joined AA

- A framed photo of you and your spouse—autographed

- A gaudy-looking gold charm or pin

- Men's handkerchiefs in assorted colors designed not to match most common shades of business suits

- Abundantly flowery stationery that you'd be embarrassed to send to anyone except, perhaps, your grandmother

4
The Final Steps

♥

The Marriage License

While wrapped up in the multitude of plans and preparations it's important that you don't forget to obtain a marriage license. Essentially, a marriage license dictates that you may legally co-habit, fight, make up, fight some more, make up some more, and force each other to deal with in-laws and other relatives on an all-too-regular basis.

Regulations in the fifty states vary significantly. Some states require blood tests, others want a health certificate, some want a certificate of sanity, and others simply want you to hop on one leg and squawk like a chicken. States vary in how long you can hold on to a license before using it. Some states require that you use the license within thirty days, while others let you hang on to it longer and even fill in a different "name of spouse" if you choose. Ages of consent also vary. In some states, with parental consent you can marry at the age of twelve, while in others you can't even be part of the wedding party until you're fifteen...and even then you have to pass a written test. What it boils down to is simply that each state has its own set of rules and requirements. Selected laws and requirements for certain states are listed below. Read them carefully.

Alabama: Common-law marriage is recognized if you sleep together in the same pickup truck for four consecutive nights.

Arizona: You can marry solely to share an air conditioner.

Arkansas: You can apply for the new "Hill and Bill" license for a marriage of convenience, which means you may both have extramarital affairs when they're convenient.

California:	Drive-by marriages are allowed during traffic tie-ups on the San Bernardino Freeway. Any number of people can marry each other at any given time.
Colorado:	The new "Drop the Jeans Proof of Gender" bill is now on the books for couples planning to marry. "One of each" is strictly required for "Hetero" stamp.
Connecticut:	License is only valid if wedding reception takes place in lavish catering hall or large backyard
Delaware:	Males must be at least eighteen years of age to even taste a slice of wedding cake.
Georgia:	With parental consent grade-schoolers can marry.
Hawaii:	License states that couple may not honeymoon in Hawaii.
Idaho:	You can legally marry cattle.
Illinois:	Required tests include VD, HIV, SAT, State Capitals, and spelling.
Indiana:	Must be eighteen and know the definition of the term Hoosiers.
Iowa:	First cousins may marry.
Kentucky:	Ceremony may take place on any day except Derby Day.
Massachusetts:	Sharing a non-coed dormitory for three days without being caught automatically allows common-law status.
Mississippi:	Siblings can marry.
Nevada:	Vending machines dispense licenses for $9. Must have exact change.
New York:	In New York City one can pick up authentic marriage license reproduction for $6.95 at Times Square on Forty-second Street.
North Carolina:	Shotgun weddings still legal—just specify on license.
Tennessee:	License clearly states that Elvis must be mentioned at least once during ceremony.

Texas:	Marriage to a horse is allowed with consent by Ross Perot.
Utah:	"Number of wives" line may be left blank and filled in at a later date.
Washington, DC:	Cash and/or status allows anyone a license to do whatever they wish.

Before going for a license it's important that you call the local marriage license bureau and ask what documentation you will need. Commonly you'll need your birth certificate, certificate of divorce, health records, ninth-grade report cards, Girl or Boy Scout merit badges, receipts of paid parking tickets, and library card, as well as citizenship papers, Valentine's Day cards and two Chinese take-out menus. (The menus are in case the clerks are ready to take their lunch break.)

It's also important that your marriage license, to be valid, is signed by at least two of the following:

1. Civil official
2. Religious official
3. NFL official
4. Ship captain
5. Captain Kirk
6. Cap'n Crunch
7. High school ceramics teacher
8. Dr. Joyce Brothers
9. State senator
10. Lead singer of Metallica

Warning!

Be Aware of Fraudulent Marriage Licenses, Marriage Bureaus, and Requirements.

1. A valid marriage license should not have a space on the back where you can offer to donate your organs.

2. There is no written test for a marriage license with multiple choice questions such as: Take my wife: A: Bowling B. To the Movies   C. Please   D. Away.

3. The license should not cost more than the reception.

4. There is no "road test" for a marriage license.

5. A marriage license that comes in a discount pack for White Castle hamburgers is not valid.

6. You cannot obtain a marriage license by answering three questions correctly on a local talk radio station.

7. Ed McMahon's picture should not appear on your marriage license.

8. A marriage license written in pencil on the back of a $2.00 betting ticket from Belmont racetrack is not legally binding.

9. A legitimate marriage license does not come in an envelope marked YOU MAY ALREADY BE A WINNER.

10. Oprah Winfrey's signature does not make your marriage license valid.

♥

Bridal Showers and Bachelorette Parties

Typically the bridal shower is a surprise (of course the bride gets the hint when nineteen people suggest that she leave next Saturday open between noon and 4:30). Traditionally a wishing well centered around the kitchen or the home is part of the afternoon festivities, and gifts are generally on the practical side, with a couple of sexy lingerie items thrown in to liven up the party.

Bridal parties are social, pleasant, often chatty occasions, but bachelorette parties are an event unto themselves. If you're lucky your maid of honor will choose the best of both worlds.

Bridal Parties	*Bachelorette Parties*
Tea is served.	Long Island Ice Tea and other stiff alcoholic concoctions are served.

Bridal Parties

Gifts include:
Plenty of practical gifts for entertaining friends and family in your home.

Victoria's Secret lingerie.

Conversation centers around entertaining in the home and what size sofa to buy.

Marriage jokes liven things up a bit.

Activities include games and stuffing small gifts into the wishing well.

Bachelorette Parties

Gifts include:
Plenty of semi-obscene toys for entertaining in the bedroom only.

Victoria's Secret's "secret" lingerie.

Conversation centers around entertaining in the bedroom and penis size.

Stupid men jokes are the trend of the day.

Activities include gawking and stuffing dollars into the jockstrap of a male stripper nicknamed "Long Horn."

♥

The Bachelor Party

In recent years, bachelor parties have gone to extremes. They've become extremely conservative and dull or extremely raunchy and wild. The best man plans the party, and it's up to him to set the appropriate tone for the evening.

Be it shyness, a façade of maturity, or fear of the bride's revenge, but some bachelor parties, such as those of insurance salesmen, bankers, brokers, and even doctors, are often nothing more than a polite dinner at a fine restaurant. BORING!

The more typical bachelor party should involve at least partial nudity, a significant amount of alcohol, and at least one videotape that wouldn't be sold at Blockbuster or shown on HBO.

Below are the two ends of the spectrum. See if your best man can place you appropriately somewhere in between. Ladies, don't worry, your fiancé will take the conservative approach—at least that's what he'll tell you.

Varieties of Bachelor Parties

The Boring Approach

Dinner at a fine restaurant.

A moderate amount of champagne and some mixed drinks

Discussion of the market, investment banking, and the best routes when driving from Boston to Montreal.

Gifts include a new slide rule, a pen and pencil set, and a subscription to *Newsweek*.

The highlights of the evening include watching "Masterpiece Theater" and an in-person demonstration of setting up an investment portfolio by a guy named Harvey.

The Exciting Approach

Dinner at a bar.

Enough beer to sink an oil tanker.

Discussion about women's sexuality, breasts, and the best routes to scoring in an elevator.

Gifts include a rubber schlong and a magazine called *Babes in Leather*.

The highlights of the evening include watching *Debbie Does Dallas* in 3D and gyrating between two buxom strippers named Fire and Foxy.

♥

Prenuptials

Some people feel that once you enter into the realm of prenuptial agreements you are essentially saying that you expect the marriage to end in divorce. After all, if you are entering into marriage with the notion that it's easy to get out of, should you want to, you may not be all that committed in the first place. Here are some reactions to the introduction of prenuptial agreements into a relationship.

☿

"He handed this document to me during dinner at a fancy restaurant. I stuffed it in his soup."

Doris, 26, of St. Louis

♀

"I refused to sign it, but I was kind of happy that he presented it. It gave me the feeling that he had more money stashed away somewhere."

Maureen, 33, of New York City

♀

"I tore up the stupid thing. If she thinks I'm only marrying her for her money, she's dead wrong, and I'm hurt. I'm marrying her because of her looks."

Felix, 37, Boise

♀

"I had no problem with it. There are so many divorces I figure it can't hurt to be prepared just in case. Besides, I've got a lot more money than he does and if he thinks he can screw me over, he's got another think coming."

Doris, 31, Cleveland

♀

"At first she wouldn't sign it; we had a big fight and she left. Later she came to her senses, returned, signed it, and we've been happy together ever since. Ironically, last year we went bankrupt, so I guess it didn't matter after all."

Max, 46, Buffalo

♀

"I said sure, I'll sign it, provided you sign a legal document that forbids you to watch another football game until the year 2000. Fair is fair, right?"

Doreen, 24, Chicago

♀

"I made him eat it!"

Gayle, 39, Houston

♀

"She suggested it and I was glad because my first wife took me for everything she could get. In fact, if she finds out that I'm remarrying, she'll probably get custody of my new bride...just for spite."

Dan, 47, Pittsburgh

♈

"At first she didn't want to sign it; she thought it was a terrible idea. Then I told her my folks agreed with her completely—then she signed. Always use that reverse psychology if you can."

Merle, 37, Detroit

♈

"He's much older than I am, so it really takes the fun out of marrying him."

Sandra, 22, Denver

♈

"Would you believe she stuffed it in my soup?"

Armond, 29, St. Louis

♈

"It's a good idea for us because I'll probably be more successful than him and he'll want half of everything I make...that's the law here in California, just ask Johnny Carson."

Carol, 27, Los Angeles

♈

"Hey, I'd never leave home without one."

Johnny Carson, 69, Malibu

Ways to Introduce a Prenuptial Agreement Into Your Relationship

1. Hand it to him in an envelope with the Publisher's Clearinghouse label on it.
2. Have it delivered with a singing telegram.
3. Have your therapist explain to your fiancé that it's important for your emotional stability.
4. Withhold sex until signing.

Polite Ways to Decline a Prenup

1. Explain that you don't want his money and storm out of the room.

2. Explain that love is not bound by legal contracts and storm out of the room.

3. Explain that you don't believe in precautionary measures in something as important as marriage and storm out of the room.

4. Just storm out of the room.

5. Withhold sex (but stay in the room).

6. Stuff it in his soup.

♥

Rehearsals

It's important that everyone walking down the aisle and performing particular duties on the day of the wedding know when to walk, where to walk, when to stand by, when to pose for photos, when to cry, when to clamor around the loving couple, when to back off, etc.

Many weddings are rehearsed on the morning of the big event. More complicated wedding processions are often rehearsed several times prior to the big day.

Below are a few things you should remember regarding wedding rehearsals.

1. Nineteen full-dress rehearsals is excessive.

2. It's okay to use a cardboard cutout for the best man if he insists on staying home and watching Monday-night football.

3. Don't fly in out-of-town guests for authenticity.

4. Schedule rehearsals at convenient times—most people won't be able to miss five working days or cancel plans for a month of Saturday nights for your rehearsals.

Rehearsal Styles

Who the bride and groom are, who the parents are, how seriously they take rehearsals, and who else is participating will determine the style and manner of your rehearsals. While determining the best way to make your rehearsals run smoothly, you might look at the list below and see if you've attended some of the following rehearsals:

The Commandant Approach: They're taking it *much* too seriously.

Ushers in full tuxedos can be seen dropping and doing push-ups for not following orders, while the bride's mother can be heard blowing a whistle and shouting, "You'll walk that aisle all night if you have to until you get it right!" The father is armed and guarding a detention center. Laughter and talking is prohibited and the clergy is praying for everyone's safe passage out of the rehearsal hall.

The Creative Approach: They're open for suggestion.

The possibility exists that you will be there all night, simply because no one has a firm idea of how they want to do this—the more suggestions, the more confusion. "Perhaps we should enter from that side, or better yet from over there...or maybe the ushers should come in from that side...or better yet..." Ultimately those in charge will tire and you'll end up, at 3:00 A.M., performing the same exact rehearsal you did at 8:00 P.M. However, they will think it's the creative culmination of 129 brilliant suggestions by the bridal party and the on-hand staff who have remained awake.

The Off-Beat Approach: No one is taking it seriously.

It's a full five hours of can-you-top-this with jokes and gags about the couple, the guests, the location, and the wedding itself. It's a great chance for everyone involved to get the giggles out of his system. Even the clergyperson starts off with a variation of Henny Youngman: "Take this couple, please." It's a laugh-riot good time from which you and all others gathered will come away not knowing who walks with whom or when, or from where you enter...or anything else. With any luck at all the bride won't end up accidentally married to the best man.

The Hurried Approach: We just don't have a lot of time for this.

For whatever reason, there isn't a lot of time for the rehearsal, so everything is done on fast-forward. You'll see the bride and groom jogging down the aisle to be met by the clergyperson, or a stand-in, who'll recite, "Gathered here, do you, do you, I pronounce you, kiss now and get out of here." Wear roller skates and pay strict attention, because if you miss something there's no time to repeat it.

The Rehearsal Dinner

For rehearsals done in advance of the wedding day itself, it's become common for the couple or their families to hold a rehearsal dinner for the bridal party.

The dinner should be at a nice restaurant, and it's a good idea to plan a fixed menu. Otherwise, bridal party participants may decide that while they're spending time and money on your wedding, you should spend money on their lobster dinner with all the trimmings. You might consider a restaurant with the words ALL YOU CAN EAT JUST $9.95 out front. And if you're really looking to economize, you might opt for the McRehersal dinner, which comes complete with toys for the kiddies on hand.

Things You May Learn at Your Wedding Rehearsal

Actual couples share with us a few things they found out at their wedding rehearsals, which in some cases helped their weddings proceed more smoothly.

Y

"They didn't tell us the dance floor would be slippery. When Jack sprained his ankle we knew. He was okay by the wedding…didn't really matter, he was never a very good dancer anyway." (Jack gives her a dirty look.)

Mary and Jack from Illinois

Y

"It was at the rehearsal dinner that we realized we really didn't want to get married, just move in together. It saved Antoinette's parents a lot of money on the wedding. As it turned out they still had a lot of bills to pay when we told her father and he had a mild heart attack."

Phil and Antoinette from Milwaukee

Y

"We found out that the best man, Michael, and one of the ushers, Perry, were a gay couple when we asked the bridal party to pick partners to join in the first dance. It was fine with us, but Jermaine's dad insisted they not dance together during the ceremony. They didn't, but Michael sat on Perry's

lap for a couple of photos. [Claire laughs.] We can't wait til Jermaine's dad gets the proofs."

Claire and Jermaine from Georgia

♀

"We learned that our families not only don't get along, but that an armed security guard should be included at the reception, just in case."

Cynthia and Mark from Connecticut

♀

"We learned that if the slowest people we know are in the front of the wedding procession, everything will be thrown off and we'll have to pay the minister overtime."

Jerry and Elenore from Boston

♀

"The wedding rehearsal was the first time we realized how nervous we really were. Many couples seek mutual orgasm…we had mutual fainting spells."

Marsha and Jack from New Jersey

♀

"Do you know what listening to forty minutes of jokes about Ben & Jerry's ice cream is like? Fortunately by the time the wedding came around, everyone had gotten it out of their system. Everyone but the two of us, who finally saw the humor in it and cracked up at the altar."

Ben and Jerri from Dallas

♥

Cold Feet

It's not uncommon for either the bride or the groom to experience cold feet on the day of the wedding. After all, marriage is a big step, one made once or twice or perhaps three times in your lifetime…unless, of course, you're Elizabeth Taylor, Zsa Zsa Gabor, or Johnny Carson, and then it's just another way to spend a weekend.

The important things to remember are that you love your mate very much and that if you don't go through with the wedding, whoever is paying for it will kill you. It's important not to think about the fact that all of your closest friends, relatives, and perhaps cronies from work will be seated out there watching you as you descend down the aisle and into wedded bliss. You should also try not to focus on the fact that you will have just one and only one lover for possibly the rest of your life. Beyond all of that, you should make a concerted effort not to think about all those previous boyfriends/girlfriends you could have married—the ones that are now multimillionaires.

Cold feet usually indicate one of three things:

1. You're scared to death of the institution of marriage.

2. You're not sure about the person you're marrying.

3. You've had your feet next to the air conditioner.

The best ways to get over cold feet are to think about the honeymoon, drink, remember how much fun the "dating scene" today *really* is, and focus on the gift envelopes you get to open when the big event is over.

The Wedding Bell Blues
(Beyond "Cold Feet")

The day is rapidly approaching and the tension is mounting. You hear yourself asking, Am I doing the right thing? Is this what I really, truly want? How can I decide if this is right for me? And that's just dealing with the caterer!

Yes, marriage is a scary proposition. And it's not uncommon to find yourself in a funk after all the planning and before the big event. It's more than just cold feet, it's the blues brought on by being up to your headpiece in stress. So how do you beat the wedding bell blues?

Here are a few suggestions for the Bride-to-be:

Δ

Leave town for a few days with a girlfriend sworn not to let you discuss the wedding at any time. Pick someone who'll slap you if you so much as mention the word *aisle* or even *rice*.

♧

Have a brief fling with a race-car driver or a Domino's Pizza delivery boy (who guarantees that it won't last more than 30 minutes).

♧

Take up jogging and force yourself to jog until you forget about the wedding. Bring food along—you might end up in a neighboring state.

♧

Take up a new hobby like quilting, snorkling, or drinking heavily.

♧

Treat yourself to a Swedish massage…in Sweden.

♧

Spend a weekend watching thirty-two rented videos in which no one gets married, divorced, or engaged or even commits to spending the entire night together.

♧

Spend a couple of days soaking in a bathtub thinking only positive thoughts, like, "The wedding will go smoothly," "The food will be great," "The dress will look fabulous," "My mother-in-law will get laryngitis," "The groom's little problem in the bedroom will go away by the honeymoon," "My father filed for Chapter 11 only because his business is going poorly and not because of the wedding," "If I don't get out of this tub soon, I'll be permanently pruned," etc.

♧

Keep your sense of humor. Play a little joke on your fiancé. Have someone in his office pretend to cancel his vacation leave for the honeymoon, then see how he breaks the news to you. Even more fun is telling your parents just three days before the wedding that you've decided to elope. You might order the always funny exploding Bible for the clergy to hold.

Another fun little way to spice things up is to change the rehearsal site but don't tell the groom's family. Laugh it up and have some fun!

♥

Imperfect Weddings

Top Twenty-five Things That Can Go Wrong at a Wedding

1. Limo driver gets lost and you end up in Piscataway, New Jersey.
2. Clergy forgets words to ceremony.
3. Ex-lover hits bride or groom in knees with lead pipe as the couple walk down the aisle.
4. Thrown bouquet causes hair-pulling fight.
5. Someone sprains ankle during high-speed hora.
6. Relatives not in the bridal party show up wearing the same dress.
7. Chocolate wedding cake is accidentally made of flan.
8. Band forgets the words to "Celebration."
9. Bride's headpiece falls into soup.
10. Ceremonial candles set off sprinklers.
11. Prime ribs accidentally replaced with Domino's Pizza.
12. Groom elopes with bridesmaid.
13. Uncle gets drunk and tongue-kisses bride's grandmother.
14. Grandmother takes a liking to drunken uncle.
15. Photographer forgets to take off lens cap during ceremony.
16. Wedding band substituted for by the Sex Pistols.
17. Someone is rushed to the hospital after being run over by runaway Viennese table.
18. Catering hall remodels reception room, week before wedding, to resemble French brothel.

19. Outdoor country-club wedding has to allow foursome to play through.

20. Indoor country-club wedding has to allow foursome to play through.

21. Groom can't find tuxedo and is forced to show up wearing lime-green leisure suit.

22. Direction cards inside invitations accidentally lead guests to nearby sardine cannery.

23. Reception room also booked for incoming Shriner's convention, and decorations include water balloons and whoopee cushions.

24. Valet parking attendants sell cars from lot.

25. Musical Mr. Softee truck stalls out next to backyard wedding party.

♥

Wedding Glitches

Fortunately "Murphy's Law," which states, "Whatever can go wrong will go wrong," rarely applies to weddings. The hours of detailed, meticulous planning generally cover all areas quite thoroughly, and with all of your guests and wedding participants pulling together with you, most everything will go as planned. However, no matter how hard you try, in the midst of all the fun and excitement of a wedding, there will be some glitch along the way. A wedding glitch is often that humorous little anecdote that makes your big day that much more special.

Here are just some of the many wedding-glitch stories that are constantly rehashed by couples as they look through their photo album or watch their video.

The Fake Cake

For Beth and Howard their wedding day memories are those of a beautiful, wonderful afternoon filled with fun and the warmth of nearly 200 guests having a great time. Nonetheless, somewhere during the day the wedding cake was removed from the freezer far too early and by dessert time had melted considerably. Although it was still perfectly fresh, it had been moved around enough to lose that dazzling wedding-cake look. It resembled more a multi-level parking garage that had been stepped on by King Kong. Thus, unknown to the guests, the couple thought fast and posed for pictures with the catering hall's "model cake," a wooden version of a beautiful four-tier wedding cake. After the "fake" cake was wheeled out, the clever couple put knives up to it as if about to slice it (actually they would have needed a buzz saw). The photos were taken and before anyone realized it, the wooden wedding cake was back in the kitchen and the real cake was sliced up and served. It tasted great, and no one got splinters.

Dearly Beloved, We are @#!^&*#

Another kitchen glitch brought smiles to the many guests as one lovely couple stood before the minister listening to his words. The kitchen, located within earshot of the catering hall cathedral, suddenly became the scene of a heated shouting match between two disgruntled employees. Thus, as the minister spoke of love and solemn vows between the bride and groom, curses and accusations from the neighboring kitchen filled the air. Finally the minister simply excused himself and headed for the kitchen. Upon his return all was quiet and the wedding proceeded as a thirty-minute truce was enforced in the kitchen by the threat of an "Act of God"!

The Doublemint-Twin Bridesmaid

What do you do when you're suddenly one bridesmaid short? A young woman named Elaine answered that question at her brother's wedding as she prevented a potential glitch by pinch-hitting for a maid of honor who'd suddenly taken ill the day before. Elaine, a bridesmaid herself, looked quite lovely as she walked down the aisle with the best man and stood by the altar. However, as most guests watched the procession, she gradually inched farther and farther away from the altar and to a curtain, which she ducked behind. She made a beeline for the other end of the temple, soon to reappear and walk arm-and-arm with an usher down the aisle for the second time. With the bridesmaids all dressed alike, many guests didn't immediately realize that Elaine was on her second trip down the aisle until she reached the altar again and took a new position.

The Pied Piper of Table Twelve

As if it's not hard enough to arrange the seating, what do you do when it's accidentally rearranged on the big day? At Eve and Tony's reception, one of the waiters had placed the table-twelve sign on the wrong table. He realized his mistake just as five elderly women were heading toward the table, place cards in hand. The conscientious waiter proceeded to take the sign and head to another part of the reception hall. Unknown to him, the five elderly women followed him. The waiter then busily went through several of his other duties, pouring water and adjusting place settings at various tables. Not knowing which might turn out to be the elusive table twelve, the ladies followed him as best they could. This "Pied Piper" routine lasted several minutes until a guest joked to the waiter that he was being tailed by his "fan club". The waiter became aware of his entourage and finally led them to the correct table.

Pink Dress? I Thought It Was Green!

Not only can guests get confused, but so can members of the bridal party. One such bridesmaid had been asked to be a part of three wedding parties in one month. Although it was a tiring and expensive proposition, the young woman was proud to be a part of all of these weddings—that is, until she showed up at one wedding wearing the wrong dress. Fortunately a guest with a sports car and a penchant for danger was able to drive her home and back, delaying the ceremony by only fifteen minutes.

Other such wedding glitches include:

The Clumsy Groom who accidentally shortened his bride's dress a few inches by stepping on it during their first dance. The bride took the new look "in stride."

The Case of the Missing Soup. This was achieved by a couple of forgetful waiters who simply served the salad, appetizer, and main course, realizing much later that soup had been scheduled somewhere in between. They offered to make up for their error by serving it, but the couple thought it would be inappropriate in between the wedding cake and the Viennese table.

The Wrong Shirt. Morris, a groom of some forty years, recalls that at his wedding, his brother, his best man, wore a shirt that was too tight around the collar. "Between the tightly buttoned shirt that was too small for him and the fact that he was quite nervous about walking down the aisle, ten minutes before the wedding he fainted." Sans necktie and with collar loosened, he was revived just in time to participate in the ceremony.

32 Morgan Road, Not 52. One of the most flowery of glitches occurred when $2,000 worth of flowers and 65 folding chairs were set up in the backyard for an afternoon wedding. Unfortunately, the planner had set them up in the wrong backyard. It was either move the flowers or move the wedding. The neighbors, who returned home to find their backyard all set up for a wedding, consented to let them do the ceremony right there and then return to the correct house for the reception, which was set up while the ceremony took place.

A major cause of wedding problems can be the weather. If you're planning an outdoor wedding, it's obviously in your best interests to have a contingency plan for a miserable day. One young and determined bride in Wisconsin awoke on her March wedding day to find over a foot of snow had fallen. Nevertheless, she and her immediate family made it to the church on time thanks to a hired snowplow replacing the limousines. The groom and more than half of the guests managed to arrive as well and the wedding proceeded nearly as planned.

Things go wrong—it's a fact. Expect the unexpected. As one New York–based "couples counselor" put it, "The bigger problem is usually how the person or the couple deals with it. If they're expecting that everything will go perfectly from start to finish, the tiny, unforeseen little problem can seem like a major one." With that, you won't be too upset if your clergyman is a half hour late or the ice sculpture of a penguin you ordered looks more like Buddy Hackett. It's all part of the fun of getting married! After all, marriage is still an imperfect science.

Be sure to confirm the date with the church or temple.

5

The Moment of Truth

♥

The Vows

The Groom

I, _____, take thee, _____, to be my wedded wife, to have and to hold from this day forward, for better or worse, for richer or poorer, in sickness and in health, to love and to cherish till death do us part.

The Cynical Groom

I, _____, take thee _____, to be my current wife, to tolerate and to grapple with, for better and mostly worse, from richer to much much poorer, in sickness from what was once health, to revere and to fear till my early death.

The Horny Groom

I, _____, take thee, _____, to be my main squeeze, to love and to fondle, for better and even better, who cares about money, who cares about health, for lust, craving, and uninhibited passionate continuous fornication till one of us collapses from exhaustion.

The Politically Correct Groom

I, _____, agree to wed _____, to be equal partners with, during times that are considered to be fruitful as well as those in which we are less fortunate, during times when we have great wealth as well as times when we are financially challenged, during times when our health benefits are needed as well as times in which they are not, to be in mutual love with and have mutual cherishing with until we mutually feel it is no longer to the betterment of our relationship to be legally bound to one another.

The Confused Groom

I, _____, take thee _____, to be her wedded wife, to have and to mold, for better to worse, for Richard who's poorer and sick and I love her and cherish is the word and then we die.

The Bride

I, _____, take thee _____, to be my wedded husband, to have and to hold from this day forward, for better or worse, for richer or poorer, in sickness and in health, to love and to cherish till death do us part.

The Feminist Bride

I, _____, take you, _____, as a husband in marriage, to have and to hold firmly, for better or I'm leaving, money isn't the question here it's equality, health isn't the issue either, it's not about love and cherishing it's about respect, and he'll die before I will if I say so.

The Experienced Bride

I, _____, take you, _____, as my latest husband, to have and to hold, and this time I sure hope it's better, and sure hope we stay richer and he doesn't gamble it all away and make himself sick hanging out at that stupid bar until God knows what hour of the morning, and I'm not concerned about love and cherishing, just turn the damn TV off once in a while and let's have some decent conversation and spend some time together before we're both dead!

The Gold-digger Bride

I, _____, take the wealthy _____ to be my sugar daddy for better, for richer, in sickness only if I'm in the will, to love and cherish his bank account till bankruptcy or a sudden downturn in the market does us part.

The Anxious Bride

I, _____, take him to be my husband, to have, hold, better, worse, richer, poorer, sickness and health, love, and whatever till we're dead. Okay, are we married now?

The Bride Who Has Small Children

I, _____, take _____ to be my husband, to share, make nice, color with, and discipline if necessary.

Often the vows are prompted by the party officiating over the wedding:

Do you, _____, take this man/woman to be your lawfully wedded husband/wife? Will you promise to love him/her, comfort him/her and honor him/her in sickness and in health, being faithful to him/her for all your days together?

The common response is either "I do" or "I will," but others include:

The reluctant response: "I guess so."

The affable response: "Sure, why not?"

The uncertain response: "I'm thinking about it."

The playboy's response: "Can we nix the part about faithful?"

The daydreamer's response: "Could you repeat the question?"

The manipulative response: "Ask her first."

The sarcastic response: "Do I really have a choice?"

Contemporary Vows

Below are some of the lines which couples of the 1990s have added to their wedding vows.

"We've decided together to promise to respect each other's individuality."

"In this era of safe sex, we figured, why not wed?"

"We also promise to love and to honor each other's inner child."

"I take her to be my main woman/I take him to be my main man."

"We are here before you today to boot up and interface into the program of wedded matrimony."

"To love and to honor as long as she/he stays fit, toned, and in good shape."

"To love and cherish as long as the sex stays good."

"To continue to love and to honor during football season and one-day department store sales."

"We want you to celebrate with us our joining into oneness in wedlock, in spirit, and in bank account."

"This couple has asked to be as one, beamed together by Scotty."

"I now pronounce you total, absolute, and complete equals in a 100 percent mutually binding marriage favoring neither party in any manner."

"To share a Walkman with two headphones and a PC with two keyboards."

♥

Exchanging Rings

When presenting the ring and placing it on the finger of your betrothed you are expected to recite the proper vows. In most cases the line is simply "With this ring I thee wed" or perhaps "With this ring I wed and pledge my faithful love." Below are some variations you might consider reciting for the ring ceremony.

"With this ring I assume you will be hit upon less often at the bars."

"With this ring I go further into bankruptcy."

"This ring symbolizes my undying love and devotion. However, if I don't get a job soon I'll have to hock it."

"I give you this ring as a vow and a promise and a pretty stern reminder that you'd better be faithful."

"With this ring I give up my freedom."

"I give you this ring as a symbol of love, honor, respect, and many other fine elements of virtue that I hope make up for the fact that it's not very expensive."

"I give you this ring, worn by my mother, her mother, and her mother's mother, to symbolize that my family will put one hell of a curse on your head if you lose it!"

♥

A Plethora of Toasts

Raise the glasses:

(From a guest)

> Down the aisle they walked.
> At the altar they did meet.
> Now that we've sat through the service;
> I sure hope it's time to eat.

♀

(Best man)

> I've known Peter for many years now, and I wish him all the
> wonderful times with Suzanne
> that I know I had.

♀

(Bride's father)

> We thought we'd never see this day,
> but it's finally here, they're finally
> married, and I'm finally bankrupt. Let's party.

♀

(Sister of the bride)

> I'm gonna miss my sister very much.
> But she's found a wonderful groom.
> And I know I'll get over my sadness as soon as
> I start moving my stuff into her old room.

♀

(Groom's ex-wife)

> You can have him.

♀

(Bride's father)

> Here's to the lovely couple:
> Marriage sometimes can be easy.
> Marriage sometimes can be hard.
> You treat my daughter as good as you can
> Or I'll hire Tonya Harding's former bodyguard.

♀

(Brother of the bride)

I'm really glad to have you in our family,
and your season tickets don't hurt either.

♀

(Grandmother)

I'm so thrilled to be here at my grandson's bar mitzvah.
Who's the girl?

♀

(Bride's mother)

You don't know how long we've been planning this day.
Or perhaps you really do.
After all, what child was fit for a headpiece
At the age of only two?

♀

(Groom's father)

Son, lay down the law, let her know who the boss is.
And I'd like to say more but
that's all the time my wife said I could use up.

♀

(Friends of the groom)

It's been nice knowing you
We hope your marriage goes all right
Don't worry, we'll think up an excuse
To sneak you out on our poker night.

♀

(Drunken uncle)

I just want to say, Rose, it was only a business trip
and I never touched her!

♀

(Father of the bride)

Welcome to the family, son.
Enjoy the honeymoon
And I'll expect to see you at the office
exactly two weeks from Monday to start your
new job!

♀

(Fourteen-year-old sister of the bride)
My friends and I took a vote and we decided
five to two that he's cool enough to marry, so good
luck and like, stay cool, okay?

♀

(Bridesmaid)
Today's a really special day for two reasons
First, a wonderful friend of mine is getting married
to a terrific guy
And second, it's the last time I'll ever have to wear this dress.

♥

The Name Game
A Subject Pondered by Many Women as They Approach the Big Day

To change your name or not to change your name, that is the question.

There you are, after some twenty, twenty-five, thirty or more years, suddenly faced with the fact that because you're married you are expected to give up the name you've become so accustomed to since learning to write it back in grade school. For many women, the idea of a new name is a strange concept. Suddenly you've gone from Ms. Summers to Mrs. Winters, a change of seasons, a shift of identity, and (even worse) a name that bears a striking resemblance to that of your mother-in-law.

The modern woman, however, has choices. You can retain your maiden name. If you keep your own name you will be thought of as a modern career woman. Your in-laws will, however, be eternally insulted, and your friends will be certain that the marriage is in jeopardy from day one.

Option number two is perhaps the most traditional and simple. That is to drop your name and adopt your husband's name. You then become Mrs. and your relationship is very clearly stated. Your bankers, postman, in-laws, and everyone sending you holiday cards will be grateful. However, your liberated friends and relatives will explain that you've sold out and are now being dominated by your husband. He's taken your name...your identity! What next?

Your third and final option is to combine both names. You retain your maiden name as your middle name. Your husband's name is now your last name, leaving you with a mouthful when introducing yourself at cocktail parties. Many an ethnic confusion has been created by names such as Angela Scarpatti Woo or Peggy O'Riley Schwartz. There is also a plethora of interesting combinations that can be made, such as Mary Kay Place marrying someone named Terry Matt and becoming Mary Kay Place Matt or television's Corky Sherwood (from "Murphy Brown") who married and later divorced a Mr. Forrest. For a while she was Corky Sherwood Forrest.

No matter which you choose, you're sure to be explaining your choice to someone, either liberated, traditional, confused, or amused. It's the name game, marriage-style.

♥

Getting Remarried

There are a lot of things to consider for a remarriage ceremony. First is: Do you want to go through all the planning and fuss you went through the first time? If your first wedding was a small affair, you might opt for the whole shebang. If, however, your first wedding was a sit-down black-tie dinner for 500, you might not want to do it all over again. Below are a few things to consider for remarriage plans.

1. When was your last wedding? If it was within the same calendar year, guests may not want to attend again. If, in fact, you haven't yet received the proofs from your last wedding, the guests are unlikely to return so soon.

2. Is this your second wedding, or have you done this so often that the wedding chapel has a reserved parking space for your wedding limo?

3. Would you want to have the same bridesmaids, or will they hate you for forcing them to crash diet to fit into their original dresses again? (And they never liked the dresses to begin with.)

4. Is your father so tired of "giving you away" that he's offering to sell you instead?

5. Has the groom had so many wives that he refers to you as "his latest"?

A Second Marriage Can Be Done More Simply

Because:

1. Your friends simply don't like your new groom/bride.
2. You look simply ridiculous wearing white after five husbands two lovers, and a year of promiscuity that lowered the moral standards of Sunset Boulevard.
3. Your kids and your spouse's kids simply don't get along.
4. Your ex is planning to show up simply to ruin the wedding anyway.
5. Your parents are simply too old and too tired to be bothered learning your new husband's/wife's name.
6. You're simply tapped financially after sending three kids to college and supporting your ex for the past twelve years.
7. You simply have no more closet space for platters, cake plates, and crystal.
8. You simply don't know all that many people you would want to invite anymore.
9. You feel simply ridiculous calling on your best friend to be your best man for the third time in five years.
10. You simply don't want to bother planning another wedding.

Customs

If one of the couple is marrying for the second or third time while the other is walking the aisle for the first time, it is proper to bow to the wishes of the "rookie." Let him or her choose the style of wedding. This allows for the first-timer to have the full wedding experience while the more matrimonially experienced has many opportunities to say, "I told you so." Thus it's even and fair for both parties.

Many traditional wedding customs are abandoned in a second or third marriage. The bride can wear any color, even black if she wishes. The groom can wear anything from a tuxedo to a dress suit to a jogging outfit with the phrase JUST DO IT on the front. Churches and temples are often not the location of choice, and in some cases they aren't eager to have you remarrying in their house of worship either. For that matter, a judge, ship captain, notary public, or even afternoon talk show host can perform the ceremony.

Bridal showers are given, but they're different. The wide-eyed enthusiasm of the bride and her friends is replaced by cynicism and "stupid men" jokes. Male strippers are in greater physical danger with these women, and often remarriage bridal showers include a theme like "Thelma & Louise Night" or are combined with a "Tupperware Party."

The traditional bachelor party is replaced by the traditional bachelor party. Some things never change. However, some of the guests have either dozed off or left to get home and turn in before the stripper even shows up.

One of the biggest dilemmas of getting remarried is whether to invite the previous spouse(s) to the wedding. Customarily, if you're on good terms with your ex, you may choose to invite him or her. Below are five ways to determine whether this is true for you:

1. Has your ex ever accelerated upon seeing you crossing the street in front of his or her car?

2. Are you known to your ex-spouse's friends and family as "Queen Bitch," "Attila The Hun," "No-Good, Lazy Bastard," "That Big Loser," or "Ballbuster"?

3. Does your ex blame you for everything, including the disaster at Three Mile Island, The Six-Day War, and the disappearance of Jimmy Hoffa?

4. The last time you and your ex were in the same room, were you separated by a glass partition and were there armed guards present?

5. The last time you had a meal with your ex, did he or she insist it was just food poisoning that put you in the hospital?

If the answer is yes to any of the above questions, you're ill-advised to invite your ex.

If you do invite your ex-marital partner, do you then invite his or her new boyfriend, girlfriend, or spouse? These things are done routinely on progressive television shows, in foreign films, and in California. However, in the real world you may not be quite so open-minded when he shows up with his new seventeen-year-old girlfriend the cheerleader or when she shows up with the runner-up in last year's Mr. Mount Olympus Contest.

At the actual wedding ceremony it's proper to have a wedding cake (perhaps secondhand), a photographer with good retouching skills, and the usual receiving line. Of course, you have to expect the guests on the receiving line to have different best wishes. Some of the comments you can expect to hear whispered on second and third wedding reception lines are listed below:

1. You did a hell of a lot better this time.
2. Sure hope he doesn't smell as bad as the last one.
3. I hope this one's got some money.
4. You old fox, she's a real piece.
5. I guess it's okay to tell you now, I'm dating your ex.

Escorting the Bride Down the Aisle— What Does It Mean

Escorted by Father	Escorted by Ex-Husband	Walks Alone
Father hated the previous husband(s) and is hoping this guy is the one.	We grew up in the sixties.	I am woman, hear me roar!
She moved back in with folks and he's desperate to give her away for good.	We're trying to shock a lot of people.	Dad's too embarrassed to escort me for the third time.
He wants to show everyone that he can still fit in the old tuxedo.	He's paying alimony and wants to make sure this happens as planned.	The dress costs a small fortune and I'm not sharing the spotlight with anyone.

6
Over the Threshold

♥

Honeymoons

The honeymoon is a special trip that indicates you're not only married, but have survived the planning and hoopla of the main event and deserve a time to rest, relax, and have plenty of sex.

Most places will afford honeymooners special luxuries, including champagne, a romantic table for dining, and various other amenities that you might not receive as more typical travelers. In fact, in many parts of the country and the world, honeymooners have special rights and even little-known laws that are afforded to them. Below are some of these perks:

1. In Hawaii, as honeymooners, you're allowed to make love on any beach, and all others using that beach must leave the premises.

2. In Massapequa, Long Island you are allowed to show up at the home of any couple with married children and extra rooms, and they will let you stay in the former room of their son or daughter (who never calls). You can't, however, have sex there, so make this a stop on the way back. The food is to die for.

3. In Greece, honeymooners are allowed to parade naked down central streets after 4:00 P.M.

4. In Miami, you can automatically move to the front of the line at Rascals Delicatessen.

5. After three weeks in Lima, Peru, you may demand at any time that the people in your hotel or surrounding neighborhood form an impromptu receiving line for you as a couple to walk by, shaking hands.

Intimate honeymoon moments.

6. In Niagara Falls, you are entitled to share one barrel and go over the falls as a couple.

Twenty-five Tips for Honeymooners

1. Don't answer the phone during sex.
2. Never stay at the home of a relative.

3. Never buy a time share on the San Andreas Fault.

4. Never deal with a travel agent who guarantees he'll book you on People's Express.

5. Don't let a low-cost rent-a-car company stick you with a car that says on the voucher SOME ASSEMBLY REQUIRED.

6. A view of the ocean should not mean a postcard thumbtacked to the wall of a Days Inn.

7. Never try to save fifty cents by jump-starting a vibrating bed.

8. Don't spend more on souvenirs than the cost of your wedding.

9. Avoid a travel agent who recommends a cruise to Phoenix.

10. Never book a cruise ship whose captain has to stop a passing oil tanker to ask directions.

11. Always spend three hours making up for any one hour you spend arguing.

12. Never deny being honeymooners—people will let you get away with murder.

13. Look at no one of the opposite sex other than your new spouse.

14. Never hand your expensive camera to a total stranger to photograph the two of you, and then become occupied in a lengthy kiss.

15. Don't invite friends or family members along.

16. Remind room service to knock before entering.

17. If there is no "honeymoon suite," request a suite far from rooms with children in them.

18. Leave your Game Boy at home.

19. Carry a note from Dr. Ruth or a known sex expert explaining any whips, chains, shackles, obscene hand puppets, or any other kinky items you're trying to get through customs.

20. Discuss the matter thoroughly before accepting a $1 million "Indecent Proposal" from any millionaire looking to sleep with the bride. If possible hold out for $2 million—the value of the dollar isn't what it used to be.

21. Certainly, after the first few days, you should send home the video guy.

22. The sex-to-postcard ratio should be 4 to 1. That's four times for every one postcard you write.

23. In a champagne bath for two it's not polite to blow bubbles through a straw.

24. When lovemaking in a gondola or on a bus, dog sled, Ferris wheel, water skis, or other form of transportation, make sure the driver or operator doesn't stop short.

25. Never leave your honeymoon early for a business conference.

Popular Honeymoon Destinations

What couples are saying upon returning from their honeymoons.

⊞

Mexico: "It was beautiful, except we spent more time in the bathroom than the bed."

Poconos: "Nice, but a little confusing. All those mirrors on the walls and ceilings, I could have sworn there was another couple in there with us."

Australia: "Are we there yet?"

Hawaii: "I still don't understand why we ever had to leave."

Rio: "Loved the nude beaches, but sun block doesn't protect those previously untanned areas."

Paris: "Educational. We learned to be rude with an accent."

Los Angeles: "Great sex—felt like the earth moved."

Santa Fe: "The nights were the best, when it cooled off and the temperature dropped all the way down to 98° or 99°."

Southern Florida: "I thought they told us this *wasn't* hurricane season!"

Las Vegas: "If we had seen one more overweight guy wearing an Elvis wig singing "Don't Be Cruel," we might have become murderers."

Texas: "Everything was so big down there, except of course my new husband."

Greece: "It was beautiful, but I couldn't understand a word they said....it was like Greek to me."

New Orleans: "We lost each other for a day and a half in the craziness of the Mardi Gras. Hardly noticed, since we were having so much fun."

Bermuda: "It was fabulous! We spent so much time engaged in 'water activities,' it's now hard for us to arouse each other sexually unless one of us is wearing a wet suit."

New York City: "It's a pretty exciting, fast-paced city. Even our wildest sex was tame next to some of the taxi rides we took."

A Caribbean Cruise: "They really feed you on those boats. We left as passengers and returned as cargo."

South America: "Everything was terrific…I even got turned on by the strip search at customs to get back into the U.S."

A European Tour: "Changing currency every day wasn't so difficult, but have you ever tried to buy condoms in five different languages?"

♥

Planning the Honeymoon

The honeymoon destination should fit within your budget, be a romantic setting, and include the activities you both enjoy. Thus if skiing, tobogganing, and sex by a fireplace are his wishes and tropical drinks, white sandy beaches, and sex in the ocean are your desires, you're going to need to make some major compromises. You'll probably end up in Cleveland. The trick is to decide first what activities besides sex you want to do together. After all, this is your honeymoon and you should do everything together.

You also should consider what type of trip this should be. Do you want to combine sex with sightseeing? Explore battlegrounds where muskets were fired by day while firing your own shots by night? Would you prefer outdoor sporting activities by day to complement indoor sporting activities by night? Or would you prefer the warmth of the sun by day and the warmth of…you get the idea.

Nowadays, people are honeymooning almost everywhere. It's not unlikely that you'll find a four-star resort in the depths of Uganda. And you can be sure they take MasterCard or Visa and have late check-in, ice machines on every floor, and valet parking.

Travel in luxury.

Honeymoon Hideaways With Hidden Hooks

Honeymoon hideaways are a great idea, but you must carefully research what you're paying for and where it's located. The ads sound great, but do they always say what they really mean? Below are some of the hooks behind some of the ads.

What the Ad Says	*What the Ad Means*
Honeymoon in a quiet, secluded mountain retreat. Snuggle by the fireplace while wildlife runs by your door. Commune with nature.	Trek your way up steep hills to a cabin in the middle of nowhere. Experience coitus interruptus as hunters chase wildlife past your door. Get bit by raccoons fornicating under your bed.

♥   *The Longest Aisle*

What the Ad Says

Waterfront honeymoon cottage. Enjoy the gentle ripple of the water and breathtaking seaside views. Watch the schooners and fishing boats set sail.

What the Ad Means

Experience the constant smell of fish. Run to the bathroom because of the subliminal message of constantly, yet gently, rippling water. Read sweaty fishermen's tattoos.

What the Ad Says

Partake of all a luxury resort has to offer. Gourmet meals, exotic drinks, top entertainment, state-of-the-art fitness spa, and personal attendant to meet your every need!

What the Ad Means

Spend every cent you received in wedding gifts (and more) on the honeymoon. Eat, drink, and work out until you're too exhausted for any other activities. Tell a butt-kissing personal attendant to go to hell.

What the Ad Says

Have an active honeymoon at our luxurious golf and tennis resort. Improve your game by playing with top pros.

What the Ad Means

Start the marriage off on the wrong track. Lose him on the golf course and have a fling with a tennis pro.

What the Ad Says

Revel in passion for three solid weeks in a secluded château on the French Riviera.

What the Ad Means

Watch romantic bliss turn to boisterous bickering as you seclude yourself in a foreign country for too long and lose your sanity.

What the Ad Says

Enjoy the thrills and excitement of gaming, lavish shows, and fine dining in our Las Vegas honeymoon-special hotel offer.

What the Ad Means

Spend your first days together losing money while his eyes keep wandering to exotic show girls in this marriage preview special offer.

Once you decide where you're going, consider how you're getting there. Short of the Clinton presidential campaign, no one has much sex on a bus trip these days. And you don't want to drive too far; it's tiring and you want to conserve your strength. Therefore, it's either a flight or a cruise to wherever you're going.

Flying is obviously the quickest way of getting to a far-off romantic destination. A flight generally affords you just enough time to recap the wedding, share one lousy meal together, and roughly plan out your itinerary for the first two or three days of your trip—an itinerary that will be scrapped the minute you land and discover that either your hotel is on a completely different part of the island than you expected, the temperature is unseasonably high or low for this time of year, or your luggage is in a different exotic honeymoon destination from where you are.

A cruise is the slower way to travel, and your ship is your hotel at sea. If Dramamine doesn't inhibit your sexual prowess, you're all set. Cruise directors are a nice substitute for the caterers, florists, tailors, photographers, and wedding planners who have kept you busy for the past eight months. It's nice to have someone there telling you what to do, even if it's prefaced with "Simon says." What's even nicer is that cruise entertainment directors give you practice in getting along with your in-laws—they suggest you do something and you ignore them, politely, of course.

Cruises generally treat honeymooners like royalty. For example, you may dine at the captain's table. This is an honor for the couple and it satisfies the prurient interests of a captain who's been out to sea too long and really wants to hear what the two of you are doing in the way of new positions and private photos. "I'm the captain, you can tell me" is an all-too-common phrase.

Shipboard photographers love honeymoon couples. They will take and sell you photos of the two of you from the minute you board to the minute you disembark. Photos with captions will be available, such as:

"She beats him at shuffleboard."

"A kiss on deck under the moonlight."

"The couple at the captain's table."

"Oops, is that her bikini top he's so playfully removed?"

"Fellatio in a hot tub, how inventive."

Yes, these photos can and will be yours for keepsake mementos, possibly even in those little individual plastic viewers that go so well on keychains.

Finally, you must decide what to pack. Besides the obvious 275 roles of film, remembering the camera would be a nice idea. Otherwise, it's important to have one dressy outfit, your swimwear or skiwear depending on which direction you're headed, and a smattering of everyday wear. Toss in provocative underwear, a few items from

Victoria's Secret, and some kind of birth control unless you're anxious to start a family or you have that rhythm-method thing down pat, and possibly bring along a book for those "flaccid" moments when you just need a little while to relax.

And finally, for those few couples who haven't yet had sexual contact until the honeymoon, here's a little advice from the AAA manual:

You've got the car and must now learn to drive, so operate the machine with care, let it warm up sufficiently, and don't attempt anything reckless until you have the feel of the road.

Beyond that, happy honeymooning!

♥

How to Know When the Honeymoon Is Definitely Over

How long does it take for newlyweds to join the rest of the postnuptial crowd as just plain old married folks? There's no set time limit, but little things will tip you off that the honeymoon is over. For example, you can be fairly certain that the honeymoon is over when your spouse starts accepting collect phone calls during sex or when sexual activity drops below watching Ted Koppel on the priority list.

Below is a short list of sure signs that the honeymoon is a thing of the past. You know the honeymoon is over when:

1. You find yourself bailing your spouse out of jail on prostitution charges.

2. You come home to find your queen-size bed replaced by a pair of army cots.

3. Marriage counselors are sending you brochures.

4. Your husband spends more time with his hands around his golf clubs than around you.

5. Your wife's assortment of sheer lingerie has been replaced by gray flannel.

6. The eleven o'clock news *is* foreplay.

7. Your spouse has started dating again.

8. The closest you get to dining out is finishing your coffee in the car pool on the way to work.

9. The closest you get to romance and intimacy involves filing a joint tax return.

10. Your anniversary presents come with a warranty for parts.

Sure, these are the more drastic signals that your honeymoon is a thing of the past, but in reality you'll notice the more subtle transformation from amorous to ordinary. The daily agenda will lengthen and the wild moments of passion will become more fleeting. Conversation will border on the practical while responsibilities and obligations come into sharper focus. But don't let it bring you down, because for better or for worse this is what marriage is all about, the caring—the sharing, and all that sentimental stuff that builds throughout the years, and that Hallmark makes a fortune from.

7
Settling Down

♥

Thank-You Notes

Traditionally, people hate writing out thank-you notes and honeymooners are certainly no exception. They are written out and sent only because it's the "right thing to do" as dictated by your parents, living or deceased. In fact, writing thank-you notes is a form of punishment in some cultures.

For some inexplicable reason, women tend to buckle to the pressure more quickly than men when it comes to actually sitting down and beginning this hideous and pointless task. One should, at least, expect that if you are going to go through the rigors of sending thank-you notes, that your guests should respond with you're-welcome cards. Of course, you would then have to send out a line of "Oh, But You Really Didn't Have To" notes and then it would be their turn again and the procedure would never end.

It is considered proper to send your thank-you notes out within two months of your wedding. When you actually get around to them depends on your mother's guilt-level influence upon you. Thank-you notes have been known to land in guests' hands shortly after the fourth wedding anniversary. These are sent by couples who thought they could survive with the guilt, but couldn't.

In the case of certain people it's advantageous to send out your thank-you notes very late. People such as:

1. Those whom you don't want to have to make plans to see.

2. Those whose gifts are somewhere in the confines of the closet.

3. Those who like talking to you much more than you like having to converse with them.

Thank-you notes should be handwritten and personal, which often extricates the husband right off the bat. "I have nothing profound to say about the creamer they gave us" is an all-too-familiar phrase uttered by the groom during his brief involvement in thank-you-note writing—which is often at halftime or on a pitching change.

Therefore, ladies, it's usually up to you as new brides to knuckle under, get down in the trenches, write out those thank-you notes, and make him pay for it later.

Each note should reflect, in a touching manner, how much you utterly adore the gift, even if it is a silver serving tray shaped like an elephant.

What to Say	*What You'd Like to Say*
Thank you for the lovely crystal wineglasses. We'll drink a toast to the two of you the first time we use them.	Thank you for the lovely wineglasses. We debated whether you bought them at K-mart or had them sitting in your closet for the past two years.
The backyard barbecue set was a very thoughtful gift. I'm sure we'll get much use out of it.	A backyard barbecue set? We're on the twelfth floor of a high-rise apartment complex, you idiots!
Thank you for your generous gift of a savings bond. We're glad to know we'll have money in the bank for our future.	The savings bond was a very thoughtful gift...Cash, of course would have been a hell of a lot more thoughtful and we'd have it now and not have to wait twenty years.
It was very generous of you to remember us with a gift of cash. We'll spend it on something important to us.	Fifty dollars is nice, but let's not forget there were two of you and it should have been a hundred.
The microwave was a most thoughtful and practical gift.	You've been to our house twenty-three times for dinner. What did you think that was sitting on our kitchen counter...a VCR?

What to Say	*What You'd Like to Say*
The china serving dish you bought us was extraordinary.	Did we forget to inform you that we registered for a china pattern, or are you too self-absorbed to ever listen when anyone else speaks!?
The vase you brought us all the way from France was a most lovely gift. We'll cherish it always.	Couldn't you have shopped locally so I could return it? Now I'm stuck with that ugly thing!

When struggling to write the most proper and sincere heart-felt sentimental message on each and every thank-you note, remember that the person receiving it will probably treasure it for less than a minute and it will soon end up in the kitchen trash bin.

♥

The Ten Most Important Newlywed Rules

1. Never go to sleep mad at each other. (Fight all night if necessary.)
2. Don't flirt with each other's friends.
3. Don't date or mate with each other's friends.
4. Never shut off a professional sporting event or evening soap on TV while your spouse is watching or listening from another room.
5. Never refer to your wedding ring as "this stupid thing."
6. Try not to make your spouse violently ill by making him or her taste five-day-old dairy products to see if they're still "fresh."
7. Never surprise your spouse by purchasing a new condominium sight unseen.
8. Never ever utter the words "It's all right, you can sleep on our couch" to friends or relatives.

9. Always have the gift of your guests well displayed in your living room when they visit (even if it is a croquet set).

10. No matter what, remember that your spouse always appears to be as thin as on your wedding day!

♥

Furnishing the Newlyweds' Home

The newlyweds' home usually has a decor all its own. The style often blends the remnants of sloppy male bachelorhood with flawless feminine furniture and a host of wayward wedding gifts. The combination of his and hers bachelor and bachelorette pieces creates a most interesting newlywed decor until the new furniture is finally agreed upon and afforded.

Here are some of the items you may find are initially occupying your home.

The Living Room

- His old area rug with her living room set precisely placed to cover the hole in the middle

- Her color TV with his VCR, which he won't let her touch. The wedding video always sits atop the VCR rewound and ready for viewing

- An inexpensive Plexiglas coffee table sporting a $900 Orrefors bowl given as a wedding gift, which sits alongside the wedding album

- Her grandmother's old torch lamp, which he uses to play basketball

The Bedroom

The bedroom is fully furnished with the ten-piece French Provincial set ordered as a wedding gift by the groom's parents. There's little remaining space for anything or anyone to fit into the room.

His color TV and clock radio add a touch of the twentieth century to the room, while her stereo sits in a corner "soon to be hooked up." His is the one that's used.

The walls are a mixture of her ballet posters, his Springsteen posters, and childhood photos. His Dallas Cowboys Cheerleaders poster hangs behind the door as a compromise between her discarding it and his framing it. Her stuffed animals jockey for position with his softball league trophies on the shelves.

The bed is the only carefully chosen item in the room. Firm for their backs, soft enough to keep the romance, strong enough to endure their active sex life, long enough for his height, wide enough for when she kicks in her sleep, but not wide enough to sag in the middle. The bed is the nerve center for the newlyweds, where they make plans, promises, love, and subsequently (to the relief of expectant grandparents) children. Oh, yes, they occasionally sleep there too when time allows for it.

The Kitchen

The kitchen is brand new and loaded to the hilt (thanks to the engagement party and bridal party) with six cake plates, five blenders, four food processors, three electric can openers, two microwaves, and a partridge in a pear tree.

Their combined dinner place settings total an uneven number that blends two patterns that don't look good together in the same hemisphere. One is the pattern they registered for, while the other is the pattern someone else decided they'd just adore as a gift. Crystal wedding gifts and a dozen decanters are secured in the cabinets above the refrigerator where neither can reach them.

A large rack hanging from the wall holds whatever pots and pans he hasn't left sitting or soaking in the sink for a month.

The Bathroom

The bathroom is the one room that doesn't evenly represent the couple. Shelves, the tank behind the toilet, the sink, and the medicine cabinet house her perfumes, eye makeup, hair spray, moisturizers, body lotion, nail polish, Q-Tips, hand lotion, and blow dryer. Somewhere behind it all is his shaver and perhaps a toothbrush.

The first few months of this take some adjustment, as he often finds himself trapped among a forest of pantyhose, drying his hands on their monogrammed towels that are supposed to be only for show. His sole form of recourse, however, is still the primary force behind 67 percent of America's divorce cases—leaving the seat up.

♥

Friends: Getting to Know Them

Whether it's prior to the wedding or once you're newlyweds, you will have to get to know each other's friends. Enduring them through the wedding planning stages isn't really getting to know them. But later you will…you will…you will get to know them.

Once you're married, these people, brought forth from both the bride and the groom's side, will play an important role in your social life. As rookie husband and wife, both the new bride and the new groom will be assessing these new-found friends, whom you will be seeing for years to come. Here are a few models to look for:

Meet Her Friend Phyllis. She is woman, hear her roar. Essentially, Phyllis, a management consultant, moonlights as an attorney for newlywed women, constantly reminding them of their wedded rights. If *you* cook the meal *he* should clean up, if *he's* going to stay out late with the guys *you* get forty-eight hours notice to make plans with the girls and if *you* unload the dishwasher then *he* takes out the garbage. These are the types of negotiations that Phyllis specializes in. She met the bride in college at a Woman Against Pornography Protest while burning copies of *Hustler* magazine. Naturally she's not married, but as she'll tell you, it's because the right man has not yet come along, or in other words, she hasn't been able to lasso one who sits up and begs on command. She tolerates the groom for the bride's sake, but doesn't like his friends, even from their descriptions.

Meet Her Friend Marcie. The fashion world follows Marcie's lead. She works in the fashion industry, reads *Vogue,* owns shares of stock in Revlon and Lancôme, and never appears wearing anything that wouldn't make the cover of *Harper's Bazaar.* She spends her summers at the beach, her Friday nights in the clubs and singles bars, and her Saturday nights on a never-ending string of first or second dates. Thus, you rarely ever get to see Marcie. When you do, however, the dinner discussion generally centers around the last ten fifteen men she's dated—not slept with, as she'll point out. Marcie likes the groom—after all, he's male. She won't try to flirt with him, but is game for any of his friends who can form a complete sentence.

Meet His Friend Paul. Perpetually unemployed, Paul likes to be thought of as "the artist." His skills fall somewhere between a writer, sculptor, and actor, though presently he's a waiter. Paul has big dreams, and big debts, but because he and the groom go back to eighth grade together, the groom's a secure lending institution. Paul likes the bride, and why shouldn't he, she's invited him for dinner— a free meal. Well-intentioned, he insists that someday he'll repay everyone for all that they've done for him. In the present, however, you'd be grateful if he'd just return your car.

Meet Her Friends Michael and Fern. Sporting a white picket fence, 2.5 children, and a two-car garage, they are the definitive middle-class family. They assume the position of your role models as they forewarn you about the trials and tribulations of marriage and children. They'll fill you in on buying your next house, going through the first pregnancy, and maintaining your upcoming family car, and will essentially forecast the rest of your marriage through the saga of their own. Discussions center around the children, old boilers, basement leakage, the children, the neighborhood changing, the rising cost of dairy products, the children, and septic tank maintenance. An evening with Mike and Fern leaves you depressed and feeling old.

Meet His Friends Janice and Fred. Yuppie Couple of the year, they can tell you the best and worst restaurants in town, and they will. Initially they'll discuss CDs, IRAs, PBS, M.B.A.s, and anything else that can be defined in three letters or less. They play tennis, jog, wear Rolex watches, and make you feel inferior, even if you do the same. They'll woo you with insignificant stories of office heroics and mention their promotions a minimum of six to eight times per dinner table conversation.

They'll bore you with stock option talk and try to impress you with how lucrative their marriage has been. They get along swimmingly since their earnings are in the same tax bracket. After an evening with Janice and Fred, you will ask your boss for a raise the following Monday morning, then call a broker.

Meet Her Friend Jack. He liked the bride before she became officially attached. He never quite got into her pants, but made it known that he wanted to. They dated, but became friends at her say-so. She considers Jack a dear friend. He also values their friendship while undressing her with his eyes. They confide in each other, but the subject usually drifts to the bedroom, where the discussion ends. Now in the self-appointed role of big brother, he's determined to make sure that the groom treats her well. After all, if he steps out of line there's still that slim possibility that she'll run into Jack's open arms…and pants.

Meet His Friend Wally. Wally was a gross guy in college, and has since matured into a gross adult. He knows every joke that begins with the words "There were these two hookers…" Wally brings an assortment of odors into the home that linger for three or four days, and he eats as if he's never done it before. Always polite to the bride, Wally wishes she'd introduce him to one of her lady friends. She, on the other hand, wouldn't set him up with one of their pets.

Meet His Friend Rhonda. The bride wants to meet Rhonda, out of curiosity. She's heard the X-rated stories of Rhonda's exploits. The groom is all too unsubtle about letting on that at some point in their long friendship he and Rhonda slept together. The bride can't figure out what he could have seen in such a wench. Despite living with a "performance artist," Rhonda will flirt with anything male, and is barred from parties that include family members or happily married couples. She is a constant source of slut jokes and is frequently tossed into an argument as "that little tramp you can go and run to."

♥

The First Fight

Is the marriage over? Did 200 people shower you with gifts and checks for nothing? Is it time to call these people and return everything? Certainly not! No matter what the outcome of this first marital encounter, the gifts stay.

The first newlywed fights often center around one of three things: money, bad habits, or bad relatives.

The Money Fight

"I'm not paying for your shrink!" he shouts in an effort to denounce her need to talk about him with a perfect stranger. "Fine, I'll pay for it myself, but don't expect my money for your parents' anniversary gift" she replies in an effort to subtly remind him of his attachment to his mother.

Excluding the "Oh my God, you're $2,000 over our credit card limit" fight, most money battles have underlying messages, such as "You're a cheapskate," "You hate my folks," or "You don't appreciate me." Therefore, if he voices extreme displeasure over the purchase of a $5 pair of sunglasses, it probably means that he's cranky about her not being in the mood the night before. Or if she's angry that he spent their vacation money on a wide screen television she might actually be saying, "If you really like gadgets and appliances so much, you should have married a twenty-seven-inch Sony!"

Thus, the money fight isn't usually over money at all, unless, of course, one of you is playing the stock market very poorly. So if you get into a money fight, jump immediately to the "What's really bothering you?" portion of the festivities. That way you'll resolve your differences quickly and be able to blow a bundle on a "Let's make up" dinner at a local four-star nouvelle eatery. Then you'll really have money problems to fight over!

The Bad Habits Fight

This fight centers around the adjustment to another person's lifestyle—which you must make: even if it makes your stomach turn. So he left the Brie sitting out in the living room for three days—you can always wear an oxygen mask. So she's turned the bathroom into an Estée Lauder warehouse—you can still take a shower.

Enough of these bad habits around the house will inevitably lead to a fight. Remember, however, this is not really a fight; it's just a test of how much you'll cope with. The question is, where will one of you draw the line? Perhaps literally down the center of the apartment? Here's a little chart of bad habits and how they rate. Decide how many points you will allow your spouse to accumulate, then check the chart carefully. If he or she surpasses the allotted bad habit total, put your foot down, but be careful not to break anything left lying on the carpet.

Bad Habits

	Points
Drinks Evian with a straw in public and blows bubbles.	8
Eats pastrami or corned beef with mayonnaise.	7

Uses 92 percent of your combined closet space.	10
Leaves wedding ring home when going out with single friends.	15
Leaves clothing around the house.	6
Leaves other people's clothing around the house.	35
Saves old boyfriends'/girlfriends' phone numbers.	10
Leaves toilet seat up.	20
Fakes orgasms.	30
Fakes orgasms during dinner parties with friends.	40
Drinks too much around your relatives.	12
Eats off other people's plates.	25
Talks loudly in restaurants.	8
Clips toenails in bed.	17
Answers phone during foreplay.	22
Cuts coupons out of newspaper before you read it.	5
Neglects to shower after health club.	50
Wears polyester.	18
Forgets not to wear leather pants around your grandmother.	7
Still buys Lean Cuisine and Soup for One.	13
Unplugs VCR, forcing time to be reset.	4
Greets your business associates with toothpick in mouth.	17
Cracks knuckles, talks in sleep, cracks knuckles in sleep.	6 each
Dozes off at in-laws house.	15
Wears Reeboks with dress socks.	26
Wears shades during pivotal discussions.	19

The Bad Relatives Fight

When dealing with in-laws and other new relatives, newlyweds are supposed to take a page from the Miss America or Vice Presidential handbooks, which say, "Keep smiling, and say nothing." No matter how much you'd like to stomp on his aunt Grace for insinuating that your eyeliner resembles that of Gypsy Rose Lee, you must remember that she's seventy-one years old and has your spouse, if not you, in her will.

Relatives come in all shapes and sizes, and are likely to say anything. While dealing with them one must keep repeating, "The apple does fall far from the tree, it bounces and rolls away, it does, oh God, I hope it does!"

"Family" fights usually commence the morning after a day spent defending your career to your husband's unliberated aunt Sally. They sometimes arise on the ride home from the cookout where your wife's parents made frequent implications about the finer lifestyle their daughter is more accustomed to.

These fights crop up suddenly when one newlywed breaks the cardinal rule and speaks honestly. "I really like your mother, but" is a newlywed battle cry. Bad Relative Fights may end, but they always leave their remnants. Always be prepared, as they may rear their ugly heads at family functions over the next ten to forty years.

♥

Money and the Newlyweds

Invest, divest, surely you jest! The newlyweds will receive numerous suggestions from family and friends about what to do with the take from the wedding. Naturally it's a newlywed's duty to ignore most of these suggestions, especially the ones from Uncle George who sank twenty grand into the future development of the Edsel.

The concept of sharing money is one that many newlyweds have a hard time adjusting to. They must adjust to sharing: What's his is hers and what's hers is his, unless there's a prenuptial agreement, which is a signed contract stipulating that the married parties are to keep their grubby hands to themselves.

Mathematics is a good skill to have when dealing with the new "double" income. This will make it considerably easier to decide whether a combined income of $65,000 will afford the mortgage payments on a $500,000 waterfront house and still allow you an occasional meal. Your math skills will be equally tested during checkbook balancing, when you find yourself asking questions like "Does this really say $165 for leotards?" You may even find yourself learning new things about your spouse. "I didn't realize that you had to have the most expensive squash racquet that money could buy…especially the way you play." Balancing the checkbook should actually be the task of the one who had the higher SAT scores in English. Yes, English. That way the frustrated participant will be able to use his or her extensive vocabulary to curse the unbalanced balance.

If the newlyweds choose to balance the checkbook together, they should approach it in one of the following manners:

1. Have a glass of tequila first.
2. Have an extremely long passionate kiss first.
3. Get naked.

This may help alleviate the tension. It also may help postpone checkbook balancing for a few more days.

8
Addendum

♥

Odds and Ends

Weddings Versus Funerals

Oddly enough, there are similarities between wedding and funerals. For example:

Black limos are the choice of transportation.

The guests can't wait to eat.

The clergyperson presiding uses the same tone of voice.

Both signify the end of one's freedom to watch football.

Both signify a marked decline of sexual activity.

The Five Most Popular Wedding Ice Sculptures for Receptions

1. The Eiffel Tower
2. The Empire State Building
3. A kind of bird
4. Elizabeth Taylor
5. A part of the male anatomy

A Dowry

A custom of the past in the United States, a dowry was a payment of sorts for the privilege of marrying the bride. Today, if there were still such a practice, with women's equality, the parents would exchange dowries. You might hear such exchanges as "I'll give you my son in marriage, a laptop computer, and a VCR for your daughter's hand and seventy-five shares of IBM."

♥

A Wedding Review: A Quiz

Let's make sure you know what to do and not to do on your wedding day.

1. Before the wedding:
   A. The bride and groom should not see each other.
   B. The bride and groom should not see their in-laws.
   C. The bride and groom should consummate the upcoming nuptials in the back of the limo.

2. At the start of the ceremony, the groom:
   A. Is accompanied down the aisle by his parents.
   B. Is dragged down the aisle by his in-laws.
   C. Is last seen hopping a bus to the airport.

3. Immediately after the wedding:
   A. You leave for your honeymoon.
   B. You collapse from exhaustion.
   C. You count your money.

4. The proper thing to do on a receiving line while shaking everyone's hand is to:
   A. Thank them for coming.
   B. Wear a joy buzzer.
   C. Pick their jacket pockets.

5. The first dance:
   A. Should be between the bride and groom.
   B. Should be between the groom and his mother.
   C. Should be between the bride and the video guy.

6. When throwing the bouquet, it's proper for the bride to:
   A. Throw it over her shoulder.
   B. Do a best two out of three to make sure it goes to the person you want to receive it.
   C. Fake a throw and drop kick it into someone's soup.

7. The marriage is official:
   A. When the individual presiding over the service says, "I now pronounce you husband and wife."

B. When you deposit your wedding checks into a joint account.

C. The first time the groom takes out the trash.

♥

Wedding Jokes

The most times one woman was asked to get married is 1,000. Of course, 999 of those requests came from her parents.

☺

How many wedding planners does it take to change a light bulb? None, it's your money so they'll hire someone.

☺

"Just because you used to date the best man is no reason to be nervous about the wedding," the bridesmaid told the bride. "I know," responded the bride "but comparatively speaking, he really was the best man."

☺

And then there was the overanxious mother of the bride who, at the start of the ceremony, yelled out "She does!"

☺

You've heard of a double wedding, but two couples went on a double honeymoon. It gave new meaning to the term "four" play.

☺

Besides the attire, why is a groom like a penguin? They both have cold feet.

☺

How do you get a groom interested in selecting the flowers?
Find a flower that smells like beer.

☺

Then there was the hip bride who instead of throwing the bouquet threw a box of condoms. The bridesmaid who caught it came up to her and asked, "Does this mean I'm next to get married?" "No," said the bride, "even better."

☺

The twenty-one-year-old newly engaged bride-to-be approached her parents. "You'll be happy to know he owns an antique 1949 Cadillac convertible worth over $50,000. The part you might not be so thrilled about is that he bought it when it was brand new."

☺

"We'll have to let it out just a few inches," said the tailor to the overweight groom. "The pants?" asked the groom. "No," replied the tailor, "the aisle."

☺

"Not tonight, I have a headache" were the innocent bride's first words in the honeymoon suite. "What's that all about?" asked the groom. "I don't know," replied the bride. "I'm just trying to remember what my mother taught me about sex."

☺

"I'll give you $50,000 to sleep with your wife," said the gambler to the new groom in Vegas. "In the movie," snapped the groom, "he got $1 million." "In the movie," responded the gambler, "he got Demi Moore."

☺

"You have something old, something new, and something blue," the bridesmaid noted to the bride. "What's borrowed?" "Oh," responded the bride, "I'm marrying your boyfriend."

☺

"She's marrying him because he's loaded," whispered one guest to the other. "To marry him," replied the guest, "she's the one who should have gotten loaded."

☺

As the couple watched the videotape of their large outdoor wedding they noticed in the background, off in the distance, what appeared to be a couple making love. "So that explains it," said the groom. "Explains what?" asked the confused bride. "When the wedding cake was first wheeled out," replied the groom, "I asked my Cousin Phil if he'd like a piece, and he said he'd just had one."

☺

What makes a groom similar to the wooden altar he's standing in front of? They're both petrified.

☺

Perhaps it was Freudian, but one reluctant groom claimed it was strictly an accident that on the back of the wedding vehicle the sign read JUST MARRED.

☺

"How long is your train going to be?" asked the bridesmaid. The bride smiled slyly and responded confidentially, "I've decided to add on one foot for every man I've slept with." "Yes," responded the bridesmaid. "But when you get to the altar they still have to be able to close the doors to the church."

Glossary: A Few Wedding Terms You Should Know

AISLE RIBBONS: Ribbons guests have to slip under to get better seats along the aisle.

ALTAR: Where you are sacrificed into the jaws of marriage.

BOUTONNIERES: A fancy name so that men don't have to be wearing "flowers."

THE BRIDAL SUITE: An oasis in the sea of last-minute turmoil.

CENTERPIECES: Something on every table for the guests to fight over at the end of the day.

CIVIL CEREMONY: One where the families don't fight.

DAIS: The important table—they get served first.

ENGAGEMENT PARTY: A first opportunity to receive gifts.

FLOWER GIRL: Child cajoled into reluctantly spewing flowers as she walks down the aisle swearing to get even someday.

GUEST BOOK: A sign-in book detailing exactly who attended in case anything is reported stolen.

PEW CARDS: Cards that smell.

PLACE CARDS: Cards with numbers telling people whom you feel they should spend the afternoon or evening with.

PRENUPTIAL AGREEMENT: The first hint that there's trouble in paradise.

THE PROCESSIONAL: The proverbial last mile.

PROOFS: 5,000 photos from which you can choose about 50.

THE RECESSIONAL: The same as the processional, except now there's no turning back.

REGISTRY: A wedding Christmas list, only these people should spend even more than Santa.

RECEIVING LINE: A line on which well-wishers fidget and complain that they're hungry.

REHEARSAL DINNER: Where some of your guests get to rehearse their table manners.

RING BEARER: Person with a lot of personal insurance.

THE RING PILLOW: Pillow on which to display the ring, so that everyone can estimate the cost.

THE RUNNER: The carpet that goes down the aisle, or the groom leaving before the ceremony begins.

TROUSSEAU: Fancy term used to deceptively minimize the bride's 200 pounds of honeymoon luggage.

UNITY CANDLE: Candle signifying that you are united. If you can't get it to stay lit, it's considered a bad sign and you might consider a quick annulment.

VIENNESE TABLE: A sumptuous display of calories on wheels.

VIDEOGRAPHER: A fancy name for the video guy.

VOWS: Promises that get stuck in the throat before coming out of your mouth.

THE WEDDING ALBUM: Documented proof that the bride looked ravishing in her gown.

THE WEDDING PROGRAM: A printed description of the wedding sold in the lobby for $5.95.

About the Author

Richard Mintzer has written four humor books, along with material for numerous stand-up comics featured at prominent comedy clubs, and was a comedy writer for WNBC and WYNY radio in New York. He lives in New York City with his wife and their two children.